Social Ministry

Social Ministry

BY
DIETER T. HESSEL

THE WESTMINSTER PRESS
PHILADELPHIA

Scripture quotations from the Revised Standard Version of the Bible, copyright 1946, 1952, © 1971, 1973 by the Division of Christian Education of the National Council of the Churches of Christ in the U.S.A., are used by permission.

BOOK DESIGN BY DOROTHY ALDEN SMITH

First edition

Published by The Westminster Press®
Philadelphia, Pennsylvania

PRINTED IN THE UNITED STATES OF AMERICA
9 8 7 6 5 4 3 2 1

Library of Congress Cataloging in Publication Data

Hessel, Dieter T.
  Social ministry.

  Includes bibliographical references and index.
  1. Church and the world.   I. Title.
BR115.W6H47   261.8   82-6960
ISBN 0-664-24422-X   AACR2

Contents

Part III / CONCLUSION

Preface

All church members share one common ministry, which is social in all of its aspects. Thus there is no question as to whether the church will be involved in social ministry; the only questions are why and how. As the social crisis deepens, will our congregations retreat from troubling events into quiet sanctuaries, or will they become "proactive" communities of shalom? By what means can parish ministry be liberated from its private, pious, parochial, psychological box to make a public as well as personal witness, to show global as well as local awareness, to meet human need with good Samaritan love while acting for justice with prophetic boldness?

This book is not another tour of the issues. It is a careful exploration of a whole strategy of parish mission/ministry in response to urgent ethical concerns. A preoccupation with immediate issue analysis and pragmatic action programs to the neglect of basic theory and skills of ministry is one of several bad habits we church and society leaders need to overcome.

Many parish leaders, of course, have a different temptation—to ignore vigorous social engagement altogether in preference for a more acceptable ministry. But *faithful* congregational life depends on participation in the public sufferings of God. My efforts to raise biblical consciousness along this line try to steer clear of both the fog of liberal prooftexting and the swamps of conservative biblicism.

Most of the book explores the comprehensive, congregational nature of whole ministry in society. Chapters 4–9, particularly, specify the dynamic social significance of all the main modes or functions of parish life.

Since nothing informs theory better than does sound practice, I visited clergy and lay leaders in parishes across the country to gain a fresh view of what congregations are doing in society and the problems encountered in developing a whole ministry. These field visits and related reading prepared me to initiate a program of leadership development for social ministry. Here I have gone into more depth than is possible in continuing education events. A book, on the other hand, cannot substitute for the team of consultants with whom I work, nor does this book incorporate the tools we use, in Social Ministry Institutes.[1]

To explore the terrain of whole ministry is to exceed the limits of knowledge gained from personal engagement, field interviews, and continuing study. Even the informed explorer must explain with novelist John Le Carré, "If I knew exactly where I stood, I wouldn't write." Writing makes things clearer, but there is much more to see. Welcome to practitioners and professors who know more about particular aspects of the subject, and can build on this approach. I hope that these chapters at least point toward a whole public witness to the gospel, and outline a congregational praxis which can orient continuing education/action.

Time to write this manuscript was granted in the form of study leaves by my employing organization, the Program Agency of The United Presbyterian Church in the U.S.A. I especially appreciate the encouragement of colleagues in that agency and the insights offered by practitioners, presbyters, ethicists, and ecumenical cohorts in social action.

Some of those who informed this whole approach to

ministry in society or made helpful editorial suggestions are: Douglas Bartlett, Ned Edwards, William Gibson, Beverly Harrison, Bryce Little, Eunice and Richard Poethig, Harvey Seifert, Gayraud Wilmore. The most detailed discussion occurred with my wife, Karen, whose experience and skill in aspects of social ministry enriched the manuscript at several points, and whose shared commitment lightened the burden of writing.

Thus I dedicate this book:

To Karen

Who, as a partner in ministry that seeks justice,
has taught me new dimensions of mutual love

D.T.H.

Part I / CONTEXT AND PURPOSE

1

To Reconstruct a Whole Ministry

Happy is the one whose hope is in the Lord God,
who made heaven and earth, the sea, and all that is in
   them;
who keeps faith for ever;
executes justice for the oppressed; gives food to the
   hungry;
sets the prisoners free; opens the eyes of the blind;
lifts up those who are bowed down; watches over the
   sojourners;
upholds the widow and the fatherless; and brings the
   wicked to ruin.
The Lord will reign for ever, thy God, O Zion, to all
   generations.
Praise the Lord!

                                    —Psalm 146:5–10

Faithful life begins and ends in "Alleluia!" to the
Creator, Liberator, and Advocate. No forms of injustice are
tolerable and no aspects of nature or human existence are
unimportant to the people who praise this God. Their
ministry is as politically active as it is personally caring, as
socially alert as it is spiritually deep, as devout in prayer as
it is vigorous in doing justice.

In recent leadership development events I have met
hundreds of grass-roots church leaders (clergy and lay)
who share this intention. They want to reconstruct a whole
ministry in society that encompasses all modes of congre-

gational life, utilizes available skills and resources, and exhibits priestly-prophetic-political integrity.

My perspective on this subject was gained over two decades of pilgrimage as a pastor, ethicist, analyst, educator, and developer of churchwide programs, who has been in a position to discern what is happening to the church's social involvement. While witnessing many moments of faithfulness, I have encountered three major obstacles or troubling trends—namely, clergy miseducation, denominational inaction, and reactionary religion-in-politics—that challenged me to rethink social ministry and to delineate a better approach.

Clergy Miseducation

The basic functions of the church are vital worship under biblical discipline, faithful participation in efforts to transform society, and personal growth in a nurturing community. In these three ways together, the community of faith becomes whole and effectively communicates the gospel. Even to state these functions, however, is to recognize that the second emphasis has been slighted in the recent practice of ministry and in available training for congregational ministry (preordination as well as continuing education).

Relatively few clergy and lay leaders of congregations are now immersed in social ministry or view it as central to congregational life. Most parish leaders misperceive this ministry as optional, but not essential. Moreover, both the many who are relatively uninvolved and the few who already participate in high-quality social ministry are hampered by narrow definitions of this responsibility. Typically it is viewed as a matter of supporting some community services and perhaps participating in occasional advocacy on current issues if there is time after completing regular tasks of ministry.

The optional posture toward, and narrow definition of, social ministry came into focus for me during the mid-

1970s as I led a Young Pastors Seminar for clergy three to four years after ordination. In that gathering of persons recently involved in civil rights and peace movements, there was little insight into possibilities for public involvement beyond direct action demonstrations or safe service projects. Most of their first pastoral positions were in small Appalachian cities or in suburbs of declining industrial valleys, where there were social problems aplenty. But they wondered if they could work for social change from a local church base. They were convinced that their key lay members would oppose it. They assumed along with many laity that a prophetic ministry is antithetical to the pastoral care of persons or to upbuilding the church. Few seemed to connect their immediate survival concerns with basic concepts of social action. (The thought that social action is essential to the development of a healthy church is still quite novel among church leaders of all ages.) They too accepted popular notions that one must contrast or choose between engagement of issues and evangelism of persons, or between corporate and individual action. Little in their training enabled them to bridge these false polarities. In short, the young pastors were already confirmed in their perception that social ministry is "extra parish."

These young pastors were in a poignant situation. Their congregations and peers were pushing them in the direction of truncated ministry. But most of them were unwilling to accept a sharp dichotomy between being faithful and being professional. They recoiled at the thought of submerging their "real selves" and their understanding of Christian faithfulness on the job, while reserving dearly held values for private life.

We must be careful not to "blame the victims" for their condition. Is it the fault of young pastors that congregations, senior pastors, and church executives perpetuate a narrow understanding of pastoral ministry or fail to show the way to a whole approach? What is the responsibility of seminary and continuing education, as well as the clergy and laity who govern church bodies, for this prevailing condition? Have we developed a system of seminary education, parish planning, and clergy work that dissipates whole ministry in society?

One young pastor commented, upon hearing about my experience at the Young Pastors Seminar, "I was trained to be, and remain, socially passive; seldom do I meet anyone who expects me to act differently." (He could also have been describing the norm for regional and national staff!) His and the other young pastors' situation calls for special intervention to develop a strategy of ministry or congregational praxis that is social in all its aspects. A social theory of ministry must become the intentional focus of theological and continuing education as well as local church planning.

Notice my singular use of "ministry" and broad use of "social." A whole social ministry uncovers the public significance of all aspects of congregational life. We are exploring a way to orient or interpret the whole of ministry—i.e., a hermeneutic of ministry. This approach to the subject differs from conventional notions of social ministries that are conceived as specialities which few pastors or members have time for except in extra-parish settings or in an unimportant committee of the congregation.

Pastoral literature typically views social ministries as elective activities for specialized persons and ecumenical agencies, or as a subcategory of the task of "community relations." Pastors and church officers generally are cautioned to avoid overinvolvement in social concerns, lest preaching, teaching, caring, celebrating, fund-raising, and administration be slighted!

My work takes the opposite approach. It assumes that since God is radically social, all modes or dimensions of ministry are social in ways that encompass both personal growth and political responsibility. Congregations must develop the modes of ministry with intentionality and competence, so that ministry contributes to social transformation as well as human fulfillment, to health of community and country as well as to congregational renewal, to local/global action as well as to church growth. I assume that social ministry cannot remain peripheral, optional, or episodic; rather it is central, necessary, and eventful to the life of the church.

Denominational Inaction

In his *Letter from a Birmingham Jail*, Martin Luther King, Jr., warned: "The great stumbling block is the moderate Christian who prefers a negative peace, which is the absence of tension, to a positive peace, which is the presence of justice. . . . In the midst of a mighty struggle to rid our nation of racial and economic injustice, I have heard many ministers say, 'Those are social issues with which the gospel has no real concern.' " If today clergy and lay leaders grant the need for the church to be socially involved, they are still likely to insist that this is *not* the *central* business of the local church.

The second troubling trend which I experienced in the middle and late 1970s was a retreat from social engagement by mainline denominations and ecumenical structures. At every level of church life, social responsibility was obscured as church leaders concentrated, in turn, on internal reorganization/administration, techniques of the human potential movement, methods of spiritual deepening, and schemes for member recruitment. Generally, the major denominations went into a holding pattern, became anxious about their institutional survival, seemed less sure of their mission focus, acquired inactionary habits, reduced their investment of resources (people and money) in comprehensive strategies of social mission. Any ministry that took strong or startling positions of social advocacy, legal defense, humanitarian aid, or political action became the object of sharp attack from organizations of reactionary members who convinced uneasy ecclesiastical managers that more than a little social involvement is bad for church business.

To some degree it was a predictable development. Church enthusiasm for social engagement has waxed and waned on a twenty- to twenty-five-year cycle throughout this century, with noticeable low points in the late 1920s, the mid-1950s, and the late 1970s. The cycles were due in part to reaction to prior activism, and in part to the need to assimilate rapid social change. Yet, each time, as issues of economic justice and world peace again came center stage, a revitalized social ministry emerged out of ecclesiastical "depression," thanks to those who did not wait for the whole church to respond. We are at the end of another cycle. An intensification of peace and justice issues in the 1980s is likely to fuel a revival of social ministry. This time, will it engage congregations more holistically, utilize church resources more competently, and reflect a thorough grounding in biblical theology?

Recent inaction can also be explained another way—as a diffusion of denominational power to regional and local church groups which are making their own decisions and keeping or designating more mission funds. Undoubtedly, decentralization is part of the picture. But do we also see a dissipation of ethical focus, with a tendency toward parochialism and privatism in ministry? Take a good look at the substance of church officer training and programs of church growth. What is their theological basis and social purpose?

Christians are called to social engagement by the God who is fully social and radically present in the world. Yet churches with a grand tradition of social Christianity have become so concerned not to repeat the mistakes of the '60s that they are "swept and put in order," free of an "unclean spirit" of activism. This has allowed "seven other spirits more evil," or more trivial, to move into the vacuum. (Luke 11:24–26). I refer not only to the crusading behavior of ultraconservative Christian groups but also to the unhealthy zeal for managerial technique and organizational process that sometimes substitutes for theological-ethical reflection among progressives. An open letter to the Episcopal Presiding Bishop from William Stringfellow warns: "In the church, as with other principalities and powers, management is preoccupied with institutional preservation and with condiments of statistical prosperity. To management, substantive controversy is perceived as threatening per se, rather than as a sign of vitality, and conformity to the mere survival interests of the institution gains domineering priority. In the church, such a governance stands in blatant discrepancy with the image of the servant community whose life is risked, constantly, resiliently, for the sake of the renewal of the life of the world."

A study of traditionalist and modernist clergy in California found no more than 25 percent committed to an activist ministry in the late 1960s.[1] Another study of United Church of Christ leaders found that activism among ministers and seminarians never became a majority tendency. Only about one third of the professional and future leaders of the most liberal mainline Protestant denominations were activist in the late '60s.[2] Social activism in these studies refers to public policy advocacy in preaching, membership in change-oriented groups, contact with government and officials, participation in demonstrations and other nonviolent direct action, and interest in party politics. If only one third were active in these nonrevolutionary ways, what were the other two thirds doing?

One must also question the degree to which, a decade later, church leaders and members accepted philosophies of self-improvement that cut the nerve of social responsibility—what Peter Marin called the "New Narcissism." The '70s spawned much interest in personal development, but again, this swing of the pendulum did not preoccupy most church people. While meeting with a planning group for an experimental program designed to integrate concerns for inner growth and outer change, a pastor from western Pennsylvania told me, "Neither social activism nor meditation techniques caught the attention of our members."

Reactionary Religion-in-Politics

A whole church in whole ministry is a theologically mandated possibility that is still in search of healthy expression. This brings me to the third troubling development—the radically reactionary politics of ultraconservative Christians. It is most ironic that fundamentalist activism copies the direct action techniques of civil rights and peace activists, and that it took the initiative just after the mainline ecumenical denominations became hesitant.

Theological-cultural fundamentalism has reentered the public arena with a prohibitionist fervor unseen since the 1920s. This form of religious activism is supported by many "evangelical" pastors, congregations, and schools in reaction to the threat of religious and social pluralism. Cultural fundamentalism fosters a uniform reverence for flag, family, freedom, and force—the four-square basis of conservative American civil religion. It has identified particular public policy objectives that at least symbolically undergird these values, and is pursuing these policy objectives in a crusading partisan style, reinforced by biblical prooftexting.

Its approach to Scripture illustrates, in the words of New Testament scholar Paul Minear, that "the more fully a congregation [church, preacher] affirms the authority of the Bible, the more fully does its life contradict that affirmation" by ignoring Jesus' commands regarding wealth, violence, oath-taking, hospitality to strangers, love of enemies, racial equality, sex and marriage, and costly service. Despite its claim to be evangelical, theological-cultural fundamentalism belies the good news of God reconciling the world and restoring broken human relationships in Christ, even as it fails to bring adherents into a ministry that serves justice and compassion.

Because of its exclusive and repressive style, this movement might better be called evangelical*ist*. Its plan to save souls from evil forces translates into a hard-nosed political agenda with simple "saving" answers for a troubled nation. With an overlay of warm piety and a palpable promise of economic success, theological-cultural fundamentalism feeds on public hostility and fosters reactionary solutions to the social crisis.

The independent mass evangelists and political action organizers who lead this movement employ professional fund-raising and telephone feedback techniques, while monopolizing most of the public service time for religious broadcasting. (The Federal Communications Commission by permitting the sale of public service time favors religious hucksters and simplistic programming.) To question their methods and message is not to question their right to exist or to present their public appeals on a religious basis. Their public behavior exposes the powerful social potential of religion—for repression as well as liberation—and it underscores the need to specify a healthy alternative.

My intention in this book is *not* to dwell on unhealthy forms but to foster a whole social ministry that takes more sustainable form than did the activism of the '60s, and is more faithful to God's loving justice than were the inactionaries of the '70s or the reactionaries of recent years. I envision a ministry that develops liberating linkages between spiritual meaning and social action, affirms cultural pluralism as well as minority rights, and is publicly expressed in just and reconciling ways. Commitment and civility belong together in this approach.

Elements of a Sound Strategy

The focus and methods of whole ministry in society deserve fresh thought—a genuine theory needs to be developed—in order to clarify and deepen practice beyond familiar limitations and stereotypes. A good theory helps us to discern guiding principles for considered action. In the words of Kurt Lewin, "Nothing is more practical than a good theory." Right practice reflects sound theory; sound theory explores right practice.

"Social Ministry" is a comprehensive and qualitative endeavor that encompasses the whole life of the church. Social ministry includes responses to issues and methods of action, but this ministry is more than the sum of the issue parts, and it cannot be reduced to a set of action methods. I have in mind a genuinely social practice of ministry approached in fresh perspective that eliminates the distance between "social" and "ministry." Several characteristics of a whole ministry in society come into view.

1. A renewed social ministry engages the church corporately as well as members individually. It builds on the assumption that there is one ministry of the church shared by the laos (people) who utilize their many resources with leadership from pastors and officers. Portions of the congregation's social ministry require special attention from groups in congregations, community organizations, ecumenical structures, and church agencies. But ministry is not something the members receive rather than do, or social ministry something that only a few do on behalf of the rest.

Ministry, biblically understood, is the work of all baptized Christians, not the exclusive work of the professional pastors, to whom the members provide support. Yet, rarely have I attended a confirmation-commissioning of new members that signaled their incorporation into an exciting, costly *people's ministry*. Would that the liturgist had said: "Now we welcome you into a life of ministry. Take your place in this active community of liberation and reconciliation. Be accountable to the gospel in all that you do. May the peace of God sustain you always." Ministry is every member's business—to be intentionally developed with corporate guidance and celebration.

2. A whole approach to ministry encompasses at least eight modes of congregational ministry, and rebuilds a

positive consensus about methods of social ministry around these modes. Each mode of ministry occurs within and transcends routine parish life. The eight modes are:

Liturgy and Preaching	Social Service—Advocacy
Education Fostered by the Church	Community Organization—Development
Pastoral Care and Counseling	Public Policy Action
Empowering Lay Ministry	Institutional Governance—Corporate Responsibility

The two columns are a reminder that the first four modes plus some service projects usually preoccupy the local church, and are not often perceived or developed in genuinely social terms (even though the congregation in its very existence is a social entity). Parish ministry has tended to privatize and psychologize the first four modes; they must be resocialized, or redeveloped with social intentionality. The second four modes, on the other hand, have become too routinized, mechanical, or done in ways that do not involve the parish. The special need with respect to the last four modes is to clarify a fresh theological focus, to give them prominence in congregational life, and to personalize these methods of public involvement.

3. A renewed social ministry reflects theological-ethical discipline. It is not reducible to a set of practical methods. The faithful practice of mission/ministry is illumined ultimately by "Jesus the pioneer and perfecter of our faith," and utilizes the rich tradition that stems from the prophets and apostles, from pivotal movements and figures in church history, and the last hundred years of social Christianity.

We are linked with a great cloud of witnesses who have gone before and, "not having received what was promised," count on *us* to continue the pilgrimage toward the city of God (Heb. 11:13–16). This is the ethical significance of the communion of saints. "And all these, though well attested by their faith, did not receive what was promised, since God had foreseen something better for us, that apart from us they should not be made perfect" (11:39–40). All who struggle for freedom, justice, and peace—who witness in the world to the grace of our Lord Jesus Christ—become linked to famous and unknown persons who participate faithfully in the social pilgrimage. Through this common witness we share the ultimate reality of worth and power.

4. This approach to ministry can deal more effectively with the changing "laundry list" of issues. Rather than picking up and then dropping each new social concern after a burst of awareness and action, we can foster continuing multi-mode ministry that is alert to a faithful vision, responds to timely priorities, deals with root causes, and offers integrated responses that are both sustainable and catalytic. Quality counts more than quantity in this approach.

Instead of skipping from one issue to another, or simply riding the latest priority concern like a surfboard on a wave, we need to build a basic strategy of congregational ministry that is applicable to whatever issues confront us. It is still desirable for church bodies to adopt timely statements of social policy that help each unit of the church to focus its prophetic action in public affairs.[3] But we need not proliferate the laundry list of issue resolutions and reports that have preoccupied church and society committees. Less energy can be spent formulating, adopting, interpreting, and studying social pronouncements. More energy must be directed to preparing clergy and laity to develop skills of ministry and lead quality programs of social involvement that express a whole congregational praxis.

5. A ministering congregation exists for others. It is not primarily a chaplaincy to those who are already members. "I came that they may have life, and have it abundantly," said the Good Shepherd. "I have other sheep, that are not of this fold" (John 10:10, 16). The *flock* includes the world

beyond the church and the needs of people beyond the immediate or most homogenous community. "Feed my sheep" (John 21:17). Clergy and laity together must reexamine the intention and methods of such a ministry, and contribute to its development in this time and place.

6. Because all aspects of ministry are social, a whole ministry in society can bridge outmoded polarities—false choices—between corporate and individual action, between prophetic and pastoral activity, between public and private faith, between efforts to change structures and acts of social service, between advocacy of justice and response to personal hurts, between sociability and faithfulness. It is not a matter of doing one or the other. A genuine social ministry, it should be obvious by now, is deeply personal as well as politically active, compassionate as well as courageous, celebrative as well as demanding, a matter of "winning people to Christ *and* changing society in his name."

A whole approach to ministry bridges the large gap that many Christians have erected between spiritual renewal and social engagement. It challenges pastoral ministry to keep them, and the other polarities, together in a winning witness to the loving justice of God.

A Telling Exercise

We can begin to comprehend the inauthentic results of false choices by substituting the word "spiritual" for the word "social" in the preceding points. What would happen to ministry if spiritual depth and development became a subcategory of one aspect of ministry, or an optional characteristic of clergy and lay leaders? Ministers for whom spirituality is "extra" would be absurd, impotent, fraudulent. The same holds for ministry that views social engagement as "extra," or merely an elective dimension of ministry. No one can be truly spiritual without also being thoroughly social; Christian spirituality develops through peaceful activity in the world.

The effective alternative to viewing spiritual development as optional is to comprehend every dimension of ministry as spiritual. Henri Nouwen's popular book *Creative Ministry* does just that as it uncovers dimensions of spiritual depth and growth in every mode of ministry. Using practical, pastoral illustrations, Nouwen instructs his readers concerning such spiritual qualities as teaching that evokes and actualizes, and preaching that communicates availability, vulnerability, and openness to dialogue. His discussion of organizing (one of five modes of ministry in his schema) seeks to walk a path between the yogi (who would only change individuals from within) and the commissar (who expects change only through external organization). "The Christian agent of social change is called upon to be a social reformer *and* a person who does not lose his [or her] own soul, a person of action and prayer at the same time. The Christian is called upon to be concerned about the large issues of our time without losing sight of the children, the poor, the sick, and the old, who ask for personal care and attention."[4] This ministry should be conducted with the perspective of transcendent hope, creative receptivity, and shared responsibility.

Nouwen recognizes the seamless web of spiritual depth/social involvement, and communicates a style of contemplative action that is value consistent up to a point. The point of inconsistency is his diffident attitude toward power. Ministers in his spiritual portrait do not exercise direct responsibility to influence social structures, but (to avoid the sin of pride) stand off from social action—from the rough-and-tumble of choosing among concrete, ambiguous policy options, or from exercising group power to affect systems. Instead of taking specific social responsibility and advocating particular social policies, clergy have "the vocation to make people aware of their hidden potentialities, to unify the many different self-interests into a common concern, to remove the paralyzing influence of fatalism, and to offer a vision that makes people see their social responsibility and strive beyond the many concrete actions to a Christian community in faith."[5] This, complained a group of city priests, is "unrealistic detachment" that soft-pedals the issue.

Nouwen's practice is better than his theory, as evidenced in his articles for *Sojourners* magazine, his participation in the Clamshell Alliance and his dramatic decision to leave Yale Divinity School to live among the poor of Peru. There, with more spirited advocacy, he takes specific responsibility for social praxis as part of his ministry.

Amid a Historic Conflict

The false polarity between spiritual and social is part of a historic conflict. For at least one hundred years now, the church has struggled internally to determine how it will respond to urban, industrial, technological, pluralistic society. That struggle over priorities of mission/ministry is worldwide, but it is most acute in the richest, most powerful societies. In the United States, the issue has dominated the two-party system of Private and Public Christianity.[6]

The Private Party is revivalistic and individualistic. It highlights the experience of having "met the Lord," and the assurance of "God's saving love for me personally." It usually says little about the claims of neighbors, or policies of justice that distribute God's love.

Churches and groups of Christians with a private orientation do not ignore all public needs, but their social involvement is quite likely to stop at the point of condemning personal sins and attendant social vices. This can lead to crusading, single-issue politics intended to crush immorality and in hard-nosed fashion to punish opponents of virtue. But when it comes to issues of socioeconomic justice, the preferred method is general moral suasion, volunteer casework to aid down-and-out casualties of the system, and support of community programs that are oriented to individual service.

Over against this tradition of the rescuers, or Private Christians, is another tradition of Public Christianity that evolved from the Calvinist movement, and reads in the Bible a message of human solidarity and a promise of world transformation. This message translates into an expectation of personal-social conversion and a call for active church participation in the formation of public policy. While working to heal individual hurts, the transformation-minded party also challenges some prevailing cultural values and public priorities, demands justice for the oppressed, and seeks to renew the social contract. Public or Social Christianity perceives a responsibility of the body of Christ to prepare the way for the full reign of God by making liberating and reconciling changes in human-social relations.

Sometimes this party has nearly identified its social vision with the Kingdom of God, and sometimes it has used church power and funds imprudently. But leading theologians of Public Christianity have appreciated the social vision of Scripture while preserving the distance between Kingdom theology and social ideology. Their political realism, for the most part, has kept Public Christians from indulging in single-issue politics even as they participate as people of faith in public affairs.

The clash between rescuers and transformers, or between Private and Public Christians, cuts across denominations and decades. Each party is actually a coalition of persons and groups who share a basic orientation, spirit, aim, point of view expressed in diverse ways. These two types of Christianity cannot be distinguished on the basis of action or inaction. Private Christians do not hesitate to act on some public concerns. And Public Christians have been known to become quiet in quest of interpersonal growth or spiritual deepening. Nor is it the case that the Public Party (the transformers) always works to accelerate socioeconomic change while the Private Party (the rescuers) invariably resists it. Each party has pushed for change that reinforces its existing social meaning-commitment system, and each resists changes that challenge this value framework. Nevertheless, each party's basic orientation remains relatively stable.

Until recently, their conflict seemed to pivot around approaches to Scripture and attitudes toward corporate church action. But most church members have shifted from biblical literalism to more symbolic interpretations of biblical narratives.[7] Meanwhile, despite continuing rhetoric from the Private Party about the illegitimacy of corporate church action, that method of action is less at issue. "The main opposition to church social action is the argument against social reform, not the argument against involvement of the institutional church in public mission. . . . Distinctions regarding the suitability of various actions seem to depend more on the specific action than on who does it."[8]

At a Social Ministry Institute in Texas, a retired Southern labor organizer, named "Red," in reviewing his personal-social odyssey, said: "You know, those conservative preachers who claim just to be soul-saving have been in politics all along. Maybe they have more electronically sophisticated organization now. But they sure were involved in the places where I helped organize workers. Who do you suppose led the fight against the union? The Baptist preacher and the sheriff under the influence of the plant owner. They got together to denounce us and to bust our heads." I asked Red why he stayed with the church after all of that. He answered: "Because the gospel is specially for people at the bottom. Here and there I've seen church leaders who knew it, and got that message across. But there haven't been many of them."

The many who miss that message or fail or act accordingly are not necessarily in the Private Party. Some of them join the party of ecclesiastical managers, who like the Sadducees of Acts 4 are easily annoyed and want to keep the peace. Meanwhile most church members are in no party. They are unorganized "independents," who can go in either direction, but who tend to support the Private Party whenever it "hooks" their moralism, racism, or economic and family anxiety. Yet they can also support groups of Public Christians when they see themselves affected by oppressive forces or become aware of prominent injustices to the poor and meek.

Renaming the Parties

The ongoing conflict in the church involves two styles of being Christian which might better be distinguished as Conventional and Cosmopolitan. The distinction is suggested by recent research on the differences in moral orientation between the churched and the unchurched. De-churched North Americans tend to reject some traditional moral norms, have a cosmopolitan view of the world, and express dissatisfaction with the prevailing lifestyle.

The church has been losing those who represent cosmopolitan attitudes.[9] "Cosmopolitan" persons tend to be better educated, more questioning of authority, more open to pluralism, and unwilling to think in dualistic terms about religion and science, belief and action, while being more willing to accommodate different perspectives in a healthy compromise. People with a cosmopolitan orientation are also more likely to have civil habits of discourse and to welcome fair methods of conflict resolution in religion and politics. These values are important to Public Christianity.

To think of Public Christianity as faithfully cosmopolitan does *not* mean that the members of this party are self-consciously unconventional. They too want to fit in, but they understand biblical faith to be a challenge to every conventional way of life. Interestingly enough, this is a basic theme in the history of Christian thought from the New Testament to contemporary liberation theology. The Pharisees asserted a theocratic social tradition that preserved their class status and resisted alien cultural influences. Jesus was a prophetic cosmopolitan who challenged the Pharisees' mind-set and ignored their conventional morality in his Kingdom announcement.

When the early church addressed the Gentiles, it had to decide whether members must adhere to Jewish law, and accept circumcision as a covenant sign. The conservatives (or conventional party) and the universalists (or cosmopolitan party) brought this passionate controversy to a Jerusalem conference described in Acts 15. The compromise decision favored the universalists who viewed the Christian way as a challenge to conventional mores, and who understood that salvation is not gained by practice of the law. The gift of grace through faith frees believers to take risks for liberation and reconciliation—to act with the same gracious justice that God has shown in Christ.

To speak of this spirit as "cosmopolitan" is also consistent with liberation theology's emphasis on the international connections and ethnic realities of the ecumenical body of Christ in metropolitan society. "To be cosmopolitan means we will engage in interethnic and international coalitions which will promote the reign of the God of Compassion and Justice over the animosities and injustices which now dominate so much of our urban realities."[10]

Congregations with a predominantly private or *conventional* mind-set may actually intensify ethnic prejudice and political reaction. But congregations which regularly explore justice issues in a biblical-theological framework and examine public priorities with a cosmopolitan focus on human-social need are more likely to act in the spirit of justice and compassion.

"The core ethical dispositions of the Judeo-Christian tradition are best nourished when (1) political activity in public life, (2) worship in a religious community, and (3) interpersonal dialogue on the meaning of faith for all of life *are found together in the lives of people.*"[11]

That they have not been found together is due to the recent theological inadequacy of both parties. "Our past traditions, particularly in this century, told us one of either two things. On the one hand they told us that questions of politics, of power, of social change, were essentially irrelevant to the gospel, that the gospel was a purely personal and spiritual encounter—a sort of evangelical rebirth that only in ultimate ways affected those other issues. . . . If we weren't told that, if we didn't believe that, we were likely to be told to believe something else, namely that we are to work for achieving power and to act through our existing political and social institutions as the primary means of achieving God's purposes. . . . Both sides of that dichotomy make the mistake of assuming that our Lord didn't speak to the issue of power and politics and social change apart from some very general principles, and that we can't really look to Christ or to the New Testament to get any guidance. Both the evangelical and the social gospel wing have essentially accepted that as a presupposition, and both have been wrong, because certainly Christ spoke and lived and related directly to questions of political transformation."[12]

While writing these pages I encountered a pastor with a disposition toward Private Christianity who impatiently told me, "You [Public Christians] love the teachings of Jesus, but you don't love the Lord." He viewed faith primarily as an experience of personal *trust* in God's love, whereas I view it as trust *and loyalty* to God's loving justice through consistent praxis (embodiment). I referred to the ethical content of the Great Commission (Matt. 28:20)—"teaching them all I have commanded you"—and observed that there is no love of God apart from love of neighbor (I John 3:11–18). Because Jesus Christ is truly Lord, the church points to signs of his worldly presence with and for the powerless; it meets Christ again and again as it ministers with the suffering.

Indeed, the issue is: What in the world is the body of

Christ empowered to do? The social question turns out to be the pivotal issue in twentieth-century Christianity. Each time the church faces a major social issue, the conflict is joined again, and different ways of interpreting the Bible and doctrinal tradition come into play.

We can learn to live creatively with that conflict as we participate in movements for arms control, life-styles of sufficiency, preservation of human rights, renewable and conserving energy systems, reform of public education and of the criminal justice system, empowering ministry with the aging, economic justice for minorities and women, action to reduce hunger and poverty and to develop more adequate human services. In so doing, we share and add to the grand tradition of Christian social ministry.

2

Every Congregation's Dilemma

The life, death, and resurrection of Jesus Christ was a ministry of God to all humankind. Through the Holy Spirit, God's People are called to share that ministry and are empowered to fulfill what it requires. . . . Where women and men struggle against poverty and oppression, ministry means entering into that struggle with oppressor and oppressed alike to overcome the causes of suffering. When men and women engage wittingly or unwittingly in oppressive actions and decisions, ministry means acting compassionately toward them for the eradication of these evils. Where people undergo affliction, pain, disease, and death, ministry means sharing witness with them in the calling to "bear one another's burdens." Where persons suffer because of their choice to work for liberation and justice, ministry means supporting them in their witness. . . . Those who minister in the midst of suffering are called "blessed." They begin to inherit now a kingdom prepared for them before the foundations of the earth.
—*In Quest of a Church of Christ Uniting* (Rev. 1980)

What Is Ministry?

Christian ministry is the function of faithful communities in response to God's grace. Functioning ministry has the character of costly service and the purpose of empowering witness. As people in mission/ministry join the struggle of faith with the powers of this age in ways that

34

express radically mutual love, they "complete what remains of Christ's afflictions" (Col. 1:24) and share "the joy that was set before him" (Heb. 12:2). Thus the body of Christ in the world continues the ministry of Jesus Christ.

Though he did not form a church, Jesus gathered disciples, gave them a message, and told them to be with and for others as he had served them. Ministry derives its character from the one who "came not to be ministered unto, but to minister" (Matt. 20:28), and whose life embodies Isaiah's description of the oppressed Servant. The Lord washed the disciples' feet (John 13), embodying in this lowly service a new social self. He became poor that we might become rich toward others (II Cor. 8:9).

Our Shepherd and Guardian was crucified "that we might die to sin and live to righteousness" (I Peter 2:24). Every Christian is called to serve the least, the lowest, the lost, to live for near and distant neighbors as a sacrifice of praise, to do justice, to love mercy, and to walk humbly with God. The liberated servant people "faithfully bring forth justice" and do not waver *until true justice is established on the earth* (Isa. 42:1–4).

Jesus inaugurated a social-personal transformation. He affirmed, demonstrated, and prayed for redistribution of wealth, canceling of debts, liberty for the oppressed, compassion for the suffering. He gathered disciples into a fellowship with a distinctive sociality. He taught that "the dynamics of hoarding and climbing and dominating, so present in first century Palestine, were to be replaced with the ways of sharing, relinquishing, and serving."[1] He posed a challenge to the Temple authorities and the structured order of the time; he pointed to a divine pattern of life together and convinced followers to turn toward this new way. But Jesus' words and deeds conflicted so sharply with established religious and social interests that he was crucified. The world appeared to have subdued a prophet who turned out to be Lord of Life. The power of the risen Christ brought forth a bold people of the Way who began baptizing and teaching others throughout the known world to become involved in history. A unique community emerged—a colony of the future.

The New Testament church developed a coherent pattern of ministry marked by diakonia. The whole body of believers was incorporated into the life-style or praxis of the Head of the church. They understood themselves to be a body of priests (I Peter 2:5, 9), or a fellowship of partners in ministry who corporately share an empowering, spirited vocation.

As described in Acts, the life of the church included:[2]

NURTURE (INREACH)	GIFTS OF THE SPIRIT AND MARKS OF THE CHURCH	MISSION (OUTREACH)
Preaching and teaching	Kerygma (Telling)	Evangelism
Servanthood within (Care for brothers and sisters)	Diakonia (Doing)	Servanthood without (Social service and social action)
Life together within	Koinonia (Being)	Life together without
Worship	Leitourgia (Celebrating)	Festival

A church that serves the Word (diakonia) also communicates God's purpose and deeds (kerygma), celebrates the story of God's loving justice through worship and prayer (leitourgia), and shares a joyful, courageous common life (koinonia) in the unity of the Spirit.

Some of the social habits of the early church leavened history through their promise if not their continuing observance. The habits included not only study, fellowship, common meals, and prayer but also accepting women as equals in leadership, including people of other races, classes, and cultures, and sharing resources communally.

The earliest urban churches stressed: (1) almsgiving or generosity to the poor, (2) support of the sick, the infirm, and the disabled, (3) support of widows and orphans, (4) care for missionaries and churches in poverty, (5) care for prisoners and humane treatment of slaves, (6) disaster and famine relief throughout the known world, (7) furnishing work and insisting upon work, and (8) proper burial of the dead and prayers for the welfare of their souls.[3] In a restrictive society under totalitarian government, that was an activist ministry. Given the much greater freedom of Christians in modern democratic societies, why are congregations today such reluctant participants in public affairs and so preoccupied with internal organization and self-service?

Dilemma of Ministry Today

When asked, "What is ministry all about?" or "What is your basic strategy of ministry?" congregational leaders tend to give uncertain answers. A prize for the most laconic reply goes to the respondent who quipped, "It's a passing phase." More typical answers emphasize that the practice of ministry leaves little time to theorize about it, or that "We respond to needs defined by the members." To that I must reply, "Then ministry *will* be a passing phase, burning out in efforts to meet theologically undifferentiated needs."

Do congregations exist primarily to be served or to serve others? Current literature on parish ministry offers tedious variations on the theme: "Keep those services coming . . . to the members." Younger clergy especially have been socialized to respond to what lay people want and to fit into the pattern of what most clergy do. A preoccupation with popular expectations and prevailing practice is actually the content of a two-volume study and casebook on *Readiness for Ministry* published by the Association of Theological Schools in the United States and Canada. This approach confuses an "is" with the "ought" of ministry, abandoning theological discipline altogether. Descriptive definitions of this kind reinforce a social and ecclesiastical status quo ante in a time of deepening theological and cultural crisis.

In February 1979, a panel of United Presbyterians was asked, "What do you see as the three most important roles of your congregation in dealing with social problems?" "Providing direct services to persons in need" received the highest rating, followed by "community organization and development," and then by "study opportunities and resources." Less priority was given to "coalitional action" and lowest priority was assigned to "legislative action" and congregational involvement in "lobbying." Does this survey mean that public policy involvement is ill-advised, or illegitimate, or that congregations simply lack experience in this mode of ministry? The opinion research gives no answer, and it would be a mistake to derive an "ought" from this "is."

Sociology of religion does not reveal what the church ought to do; it can only illumine what has been going on, and sometimes why. The better research on local church social involvement suggests three factors that impel congregations to limit or ignore social ministry: (1) Most local churches emphasize the cultivation of personal faith and pay much less attention to the social concerns of the community or society. (2) Most lay people want their congregations to focus on personal faith and enrichment more than on social concerns. (3) In most congregations there is little linkage or integration of the two great commandments—vertical relationship with God and horizontal relation to neighbors.[4]

This pattern persists because first, contemporary society expects the church to specialize in the private sphere; second, the threefold pattern mentioned above is mutually reinforcing; third, there is widespread acceptance of "myths" that justify noninvolvement. Some of the more prominent myths are "Social action alienates members" (though it turns out that only some kinds of action are even controversial); "Attitude change must happen before we can become involved" (though there is increasing evidence that behavioral change probably affects attitude change more than vice versa); and "We just restored balance after too much activism" (though several studies show that people often join the church or increase their financial support because they see religion being relevant to societal and community issues).

This analysis suggests that "if local churches are to be more involved in social concerns, the following things must happen: more activities dealing with social concerns would have to be incorporated into church programming; efforts would have to be made to elevate social concerns in the priorities of church members and to integrate vertical and horizontal beliefs; and the myths which have supported non-involvement would have to be challenged."[5] In addition, more clergy and lay leaders must acquire a clear conception of whole ministry in society, and skills to develop it locally. This underscores a need for a fully social theology to orient parish praxis.

A Careful Inquiry

In a lengthy, posthumously published study of the (campus) ministry, Kenneth Underwood started to sketch a usable theory of ministry on which we can build. Underwood bemoaned the fact that "American Protestantism seems at present to occupy a halfway house in which no satisfactory relationship has been found between its deep concern for the whole person and for the public order." With depth of theological-sociological insight, he outlined four "historic modes" of ministry: pastoral care and counseling, prophetic and teaching inquiry, priestly and preaching activity, governing and administration, showing their relationship to the threefold offices of Christ as Prophet, Priest, and King. In Underwood's study, "ministry is Christian faith in action"[6]; these are the modes by which the believing community makes known the being and doing of God in the world, and the response expected of human beings. A whole ministry is pastoral, prophetic, priestly, and governing—done together with professional competence.

Underwood noted that the charcteristics of a *professional* correspond respectively to the four modes of ministry: concern for persons, values and basic theory, specialized skills, and public responsibility. But many professionals, including professional ministers, have become narrow and fragmenting in their effect on society due to specialization and secularization. The result is an intensified vocational crisis; ministers (and many other professionals) are trained to work "with *ideas* and *individuals* rather than with the responsible use of power in the structures of society."[7]

> The new occasion the churches confront might best be characterized as a time in which all historic, primary modes of ministry are now mandatory wherever the church exists in full witness to the work of its Lord—mandatory not in the actions of individual pastors, but in full consort. The next decade may be chiefly a struggle to go beyond the most debilitating marks of secularization—a technically and denominationally fragmented ministry—to social policies of the churches that imaginatively and compassionately bring all the resources of ministry to bear on the spiritual and moral problems of particular constituencies and institutions in society.[8]

While Underwood understood multi-mode ministry to be the *corporate* responsibility of every unit of the church, his study examined the behavior of campus ministers in each mode and compared their approach to that of parish ministers. Similarities are more apparent than differences. Both campus and parish ministers are much more likely to do counseling and to lead worship than they are to undertake prophetic inquiry or to become directly involved in an issue of public governance. Their pastoral activity is primarily individual-oriented and includes such actions as prayer, counseling, visitation, funerals. Their priestly activity features leadership of public worship, administration of the Sacraments, interpretation of belief and doctrine, and reinforcement of familiar ethical norms. Clergy generally enjoy such activity much more than they enjoy working on problems of governance that entail a use of institutional authority and power for social change, or that involve direct efforts to influence community groups. Neither parish nor campus ministers are inclined to lead in exploring the realities, or to involve themselves organizationally in the exercise, of power,[9] even when they see where power is being exercised.

The pattern will change only as activity in all four modes is refocused.

1. *Pastoral care* must encompass substructures of community as well as opportunities for individual counseling. "Can a pastoral ministry be developed which effectively helps the complex academic and research structures of the university better serve the personal needs of students and helps them share responsibility?"[10] The same question applies to participants in the workplaces of business, industry, government, and the church.

2. *Priestly and preaching activity* must communicate more directly with the "somewhat involved" constituencies so as to affirm responsible creativity and to elicit faithful commitment, while allowing doctrinal doubt and latitude in life-style. If laity are to be activated for ministry in the modern city, then the new wine of the gospel must be poured into new wineskins. A ministry of ferment in the social order requires new vessels, forms, and norms of priestly action.

3. *Prophetic inquiry* is nurtured by the free association of believers who utilize the historic resources of the church in combination with responsible contemporary disciplines of inquiry to search out and clearly interpret the will of God in particular situations. Prophetic inquiry fuses information and ethical values into patterns of coherence, meaning, and loyalty consistent with Christian faith. "Prophetic inquiry combines waiting, investigation, and

confrontation." In this it differs from nineteenth-century evangelistic forms of persuasion. Instead, "prophetic inquiry is developed in organizations of the church which are not asking for the quick decision or solution of communication about a social problem, but rather for ways of participating in a continuing process of learning that reflects the complexity and depth of division between racial groups, specializations, and professions in our society and the cost of nurturing healing action in whole systems and institutions of modern society."[11]

4. *Governance* tests truth and wisdom in the fires of politics and administration. Governance is involved with forces, structures, relationships, and technical data that shape whole institutions. "Governance is the exercise of power in the structures and loyalties of a society or people; it is rooted in the statutes, functions, and authority of a society's organizations and associations." Governing in the tradition of Christ as Lord or King requires "that fundamental humanity be guaranteed to all and that this covenant be built into the major institutions and social processes."[12]

A ministry of governance discerns how community power is really exercised, and works for the public good that transcends the demands of powerful interest groups. "To claim to be a Christian who loves God and neighbor and not to attempt to be an effective person in the formation of just social policies is to talk nonsense in the modern world," concluded Underwood.

Underwood saw that authentic ministry encompasses prophetic inquiry and public governance as much as it requires genuine pastoral care and proclamation of the Word. Underwood laid a conceptual foundation for building an integrated *congregational* ministry in *specific* modes.

Leadership in Full Ministry

Integrated social ministry will develop locally and extensively to the extent that congregational leaders face directly and resolve creatively the perennial conflict over "different conceptions of the minister's work and the content of the church's program. . . . Ministers place their highest values on their roles as preacher and prophet; the laity esteem the minister's priestly and pastoral roles above all others."[13] Clergy feel considerable tension between what they are called to do and what they actually spend their time doing. "Most ministers see themselves primarily as preachers and pastors; they find themselves functioning for the most part as administrators and organizers. They also like to see themselves as champions of social justice, a role which ranks among the lowest for the laity, but they admit to spending very little time in this way."[14]

Lay persons for the most part view the church as a setting in which to meet personal and family-centered needs. They are unlikely to value ministry concerned with social ethics and public affairs unless they (the laity) experience theological study and positive social action that breach the walls of conventional thinking and cultural isolation.

How can congregational uneasiness about social ministry be overcome, and clashing clergy-lay expectations be resolved without on the one hand merely offering the members whatever services they want, or on the other hand simply demanding that they adhere to the "real purpose of the church"? The key, suggests one organizational consultant, is for each congregation's leaders to concentrate on the church's *primary task*—the transforming transaction between the enterprise and its environment. "When we examine a live organization, what we notice is that it receives materials, services, energy—a variety of inputs—from its environment, transforms these inputs in some fashion, and then exports the finished product or service back into the environment."[15] Both clergy and laity are now too "output" oriented and not yet attuned to the ecology of ministry. Mutual attention should be directed to the primary task or movement "from what, by what, to what?" The primary task is to enable both individuals and institutions to move from idolatry to repentance and responsible freedom in a community that embodies the loving justice of Jesus Christ.

A "dual possibility for service" to individual well-being and to social justice comes into view as the focus of clergy and lay action. This mutual ministry can overcome mutual intimidation wherein laity who want comfort and affirmation are threatened by social involvement, and clergy who want social action are frustrated by lay reaction. Debilitating conflict over the essential work of ministry and operational powerlessness, which results from that conflict, are displaced by an empowering consensus. This especially benefits clergy and laity who are ethically-oriented but have been socially inactive (a much larger group than self-designated "activists").[16]

A growing number of laity are actually on pilgrimage toward a more significant social ministry and are looking for support from clergy and the rest of the congregation. This has become quite apparent to me in leadership development events as participants share their personal-social odysseys (beginning with the question: "What got you and keeps you socially involved?"). The interviews frequently bring out these key factors: exposure learnings in early and mature years, encounter with other cultures and ideologies, personal experience or awareness of oppression, the example of admired leaders in congregation and community, fresh theological insight into God's purpose and the church's mission, participation in unfamiliar forms of action, finding a supportive community, and knowing particular "successes" or moments of effectiveness.

Most of us start out as uninvolved laity with limited notions of mission/ministry, or as young persons oblivious to major injustices. Sooner or later we encounter dissonant social realities, often through exposure to another culture, race, or class, and participation in groups that foster critical consciousness. A creative church leader may teach us experientially that action for justice is central to the biblical witness.

We push others in the congregation to join us in pilgrimage. Ambivalence or opposition on the part of local church or community leaders arouses our anger. We identify with movements to end oppression, or we experience oppressive reaction ourselves. Throughout we seek and sometimes find supportive groups of Christians who for periods of time sustain us. And occasionally we know the thrill of helping change to happen. A significant leadership role is to enable others to join this pilgrimage into full social ministry.

To join the historical struggle for justice and to mediate the abundant life, congregations need, and their leaders can affirm, sufficient internal tension to enliven ministry. "This need for tension—both for a congregation's adaptation to change and the realization of its purposes as a community of Christians—creates the most critical power issue of all for the pastor. It is his or her basic task to see that a creative level of tension is sustained."[17] Life-enhancing leadership is ecological, organic, spiritually and socially competent, alert to the formation of a fresh corporate consensus about mission priorities, and eager for collaboration between clergy and laity in the work of ministry. (In Rollo May's terms, it is a ministry of power *with* them.)

"What is of immediate short-range importance is to establish the confidence of pastors that they are not helpless, that they can develop the capacity to work out models of leadership that resolve questions of power, despite the fact that so much of it puts extraordinary demands on their personal resources."[18] In particular, pastors must face up to the extraordinary *anxiety* that is engendered by their structural dependence on the voluntary support of church members who want to be served, and the approval of a bishop (or conference, district, presbytery executive) who tends to be preoccupied with a smoothly running institution.

Clergy frequently attempt to resolve the stress by choosing to be "inactive" or "reactive" leaders who concentrate on the details of parish maintenance or the needs of individual parishioners, setting aside work for social justice. But they can choose to be "proactive" and "integrative" leaders who are concerned for the larger community to which the congregation belongs and responsive to the human impact of social change.[19]

Recovery of the power to lead is essential to the reconstruction of parish social ministry, as illustrated in some self-aware comments addressed to me by the pastor of a large congregation.

I agree with your statement of the church's three basic purposes: vital worship under biblical discipline, personal growth in a nurturing community, and faithful participation in efforts to transform society. I recognize that I have slighted the third purpose.

My frustration is due in large part to the absence of any clear strategy for social ministry, the lack of a consistent emphasis upon the corporate social implications of the Christian message, and a failure of nerve in the face of what I perceived to be a negative attitude toward social change in the congregation which I serve.

I do not subscribe to a privatistic (or purely pietistic) expression of faith. Indeed, I see the church's business to be both a modeling of God's love-justice in the world and a working for the extension of love-justice to all persons. But my practice of ministry has not been congruent with my basic theological understanding. I have been too structurally dependent and "reactive." I have worked hard at being a facilitator, offering a strong model of pastoral care and concern, and at managing a large, attitudinally diverse congregation by de-emphasizing significant value differences among the members.

The structure of our congregation's life, and my way of relating to it, exacerbated the problem. Of the five major departments of our Church Council, only one, Outreach, specifically carries a social ministry agenda. It has consistently been our weakest, most underdeveloped area of ministry, and I have related to it only indirectly, leaving most of that work up to an associate who recently resigned.

Whereas in a former, smaller parish I was a liberal community leader (though I did little power-sharing with the laity), in my current parish I have not found the mechanisms or the will to energetically develop social ministry as a major aspect of congregational life or as the context of ministry. My sense of jeopardy has restrained me from making forceful efforts toward a change in agenda and style. The congregation has responded to some noncontroversial human needs, but operating out of a weak structure, with confused and uncertain leadership, we have done little to confront and deal with social conditions. Meanwhile I felt I was losing touch with something vital in myself.

Now that I perceive a crucial choice, I am asking the key lay leader of our parish council for an informal conference with the other lay leaders and staff to discuss where we are and intend to go. I have indicated that I have been less than fully myself in emphasis and style of ministry, and want to talk it over honestly to see if we can reach a fresh understanding of our ministry together.

3

Response to Social Crisis

A watershed is now upon us in all industrial societies, those more appropriately defined as overdeveloped societies. Symptoms include energy problems coupled with inflation, recession and a new disease that the economists—because they don't understand it—call stagflation. . . . We are now in a great transition period, in which we must adapt and restructure our society and our economy for a different kind of future.
—Hazel Henderson, "Creating Alternate
Future: The Politics of Reconceptualization"

DISCERNING OUR CONDITION

The times perplex and unnerve us; our institutions frustrate and immobilize more often than they respond to deepening crisis. As complex and crucial social dilemmas accumulate, we wonder what kind of future confronts society and church. Is it only foreboding or also promising? The future offers a fascinating mix of given trends, predictable problems, and possible events. Apparently, the greatest of these three is "possible events" (as in the Delphi method of forecasting, where individual experts are asked to state probable developments in terms of future events, and the results are tabulated to show a consensus).

In our projections of possible events, we need to adopt the historians' healthy respect for factors of contingency

48

and decision. Historians perceive each event as a combination of contingent factors unique to that situation, and the insight, decision, policy, and action of the people involved.[1] Social trends take shape as ideas catch fire, as people's movements push for change, as political-economic decisions gain momentum, and as technological/organizational initiatives become institutionalized.

A Mosaic Future

Recognition that the future is open, eventful, and culturally shaped dovetails with the realization that the future is mosaically incoherent. If futurists once "knew" which way the world was headed, most are now modestly uncertain, exhibiting a somber sense of grim probabilities. The shift of mood marks an abrupt change in Western thinking which, until the 1970s, pivoted on the idea of inevitable social progress. The social good was predicated on further development of benign technology. The science of futurology rested on a "basic methodological premise of technological determinism and the vision of a future of scientifically conditioned bliss."[2] The futurist religion celebrated happy, everlasting redemption through the beneficence of science and technology.

Now in the last fifth of the twentieth century, the future isn't what it used to be. "Simple faith in automatic progress through the agency of unfettered science and technology is largely a thing of the past."[3] Instead, we can anticipate an incoherent future where many alternatives coexist uneasily in a mosaic. There are numerous sociological indicators of incoherence—i.e., of juxtaposed social forms, political institutions, cultural norms, economic conditions, technological choices. The future really is dialectical—full of contradictory possibilities.

Consider the sharpened pluralism of values and lifestyles exhibited by different religious, racial, ethnic, and economic groups. Note the range of public concern about family life and sexuality.

Ponder the diametrically opposed efforts to develop massive and toxic energy technologies based on uranium, coal, and petroleum versus grass-roots development of localized, benign energy systems that carefully utilize sun, wind, water, and earth.

Consider the confusing results of populist distrust of remote political institutions coupled with the tax revolt which undercuts basic community services and opposes social innovation. Note the trend toward increased equal opportunity and racial integration among the educated versus the resegregation or deprivation of all who lack job skills and opportunity.

Ponder the widening global per capita GNP gap between rich and poor, currently estimated at 11:1 or 12:1, and the yawning gap within poor countries that has reduced the purchasing power of the poorest 40 percent despite overall societal growth. Notice the disproportionate use of scarce resources by the rich countries of the North relative to their population, perhaps at a ratio of 15:1 on a per capita basis, affecting price and availability of resources required to meet basic needs.[4]

Consider the intensification of arms race behavior, including nuclear weapons innovations by superpowers, the spread of nuclear capabilities to many more countries, and the rise of arms spending for the sake of "national security and world peace," even as large-scale collective violence erupts in many poor sectors of the world.

Thus we begin to see the dimensions of the deepening social crisis which involves more than one contradiction after another. There is an underlying condition to be discerned and named. A clue is offered by Peter Drucker who, though wary of specific predictions, proposes we face an Age of Discontinuity in world economy, technology, and politics, and "while we have been finishing the great nineteenth-century economic edifice, the foundations have shifted under our feet."[5] We face a crucial choice, asserts a former prime minister of the Netherlands, "between sticking to our present system, which is largely guided and manipulated for the benefit of the rich countries and classes, and opting for a system directed towards finding solutions to the problems of an equitable division of income and property, or scarcity of natural resources and of despoliation of the environment."[6] Development ethicist Denis Goulet looks critically at the "global village" and concludes: "We see an international economic order designed by the rich largely for the benefit of the rich. The basis for exchanges of all kinds—ideas, goods and personnel—is commercial, responsive not to need or to social responsibility but to effective purchasing power."[7]

We live now in a post-industrial, post-affluent world of scarce resources, corporate giantism, and distribution struggles. The politics of distribution in austere times become "nasty zero-sum games for real money. Like a high-stakes poker game, the gains of the winners thin the wallets of the losers."[8] The primary threat ethically is the indifference of the winners (the rich and powerful) toward the losers (the poor and powerless), on the basis of which the winners can justify unparalleled patterns of cruelty toward the losers.

Conditions of poverty, dependence, and privation threaten to condemn more and more inhabitants of the world to a social "death in life" that can be as excruciating, pervasive, and devastating in developing countries as nuclear war. But the threat of deprivation is not just "over there." Especially at stake in overdeveloped societies like the United States are policies that assure the right to food, shelter, education, health, adequate incomes and tax equity for hourly workers, pensions and health benefits for older persons, equal opportunity in employment and education for disadvantaged groups, a fair balance between wage and price controls. "The current character of economic and social policy will persist only as long as the losers—blacks, Hispanics, women [older persons, unorganized workers] and trade unionists—are passive."[9]

An increasing disparity of economic condition underscores the distributive justice crisis in rich as well as poor countries. The middle portion of the U.S. population with incomes and assets ranging from 30 percent below the median to 30 percent above the median holds about half of the total national wealth, whereas the middle group holds barely a third of the national wealth in Latin-American countries. But our larger middle strata does not resolve the plight of the poor, who are in danger of becoming a permanent underclass as inflation and joblessness pauperize more people. In *both* the United States and Latin America, the lowest income 20 percent of the population have less than 5 percent of the wealth. Meanwhile, the highest income 20 percent of the U.S. population have over 45 percent of the wealth and the top 20 percent of the Latin-American population have over 62 percent of the wealth.[10] Obviously, in all parts of the Western Hemisphere including its richest country, there is urgent need for effective mechanisms to transfer resources and power from the affluent to those who lack bare sufficiency.

The Over/Underdeveloped Society

Economic indicators like the above point to a pervasive social condition of *over/under development*. To speak of over/under developed society is to locate and name the basic pattern in which so many current public problems arise. In this social condition, "more means worse"; that is, more of the same policies that produced the rich/poor gap means even worse conditions for many people.

In an overdeveloped society the food we eat, the air we breathe, the water we drink, the cities and office buildings we inhabit, the enterprises from which we profit, the products we consume, the lives we lead contaminate or undermine both body and spirit in pervasive ways.

A world of simultaneous overdevelopment and underdevelopment has "gone too far in producing nonessential luxuries and in egoistic individualism. In these respects because we continue to overshoot, we will collapse. We have not gone far enough in public education and health, psychological growth, social justice, and spiritual sensitivity. If in these ways we continue to *under*shoot, we will also collapse."[11]

Beyond immediate occupational and public health hazards, the overdeveloped society wastes large quantities of resources on fashions, luxury consumption, planned obsolescence, and weapons. Its heavy military expenditures to defend existing systems and to foster economic "growth" are socially pathological. The ideology that justifies the enterprises of overdevelopment increases class cleavage and permits an assault on the poor. Overdevelopment creates deep pockets of poverty as well as high levels of inflation and unemployment. Overdevelopment relies on, and increases, underdevelopment where 85 percent of the world's resources are being used for the benefit of less than 20 percent of the world's population.

Another sign of overdevelopment is the condition of the most powerful cities in the richest countries—marked with deteriorated housing, choked with pollution, burdened with poverty, and haunted by crime. (For example, Washington, D.C., is an underdeveloped community at the site of an overdeveloped government that does not deal with its unusually high rates of infant mortality and functional illiteracy, two measures of failure to meet basic human needs.)

Older cities and industrial regions, rather than being charity cases, are actually being milked of taxes and of financial assets by government policy and commercial interests, and are left as dumping grounds for workers whose plants were closed, for people who have been driven off of small farms, and for undocumented aliens. The overdeveloped society begins to take on some of the same dynamics as have the underdeveloped countries. As Richard Barnet and Ronald Mueller put it in *Global Reach*, we, too, are being "Latin Americanized." This phenomenon extends beyond metropolis to town and country areas which are colonized for commercial purposes and which also experience corrupt government, rising rates of crime, increasing drug abuse, loss of neighborliness, lack of community initiative, hints of despair and alienation. To summarize its characteristics, the overdeveloped society:

—Relies on capital- and energy-intensive technological "progress."
—Generates poverty and assaults the poor.
—Bullies nature in a way that severely damages the human habitat.
—Produces wrongly and consumes indulgently.
—Alienates persons from community, work, and politics.
—Wastes the talents and energy of the young and old.
—Substitutes therapeutic services for social justice.
—Fosters artificial intimacy and voyeurism.
—Robs people of social participation by means of organization, communication, and control that violate human rights.
—Generates unjust concentrations of corporate wealth and power that maximize short-term profit at the expense of community enterprises.
—Spends disproportionate resources for national security and armaments.

The United States is but one First World example of the overdeveloped society; "advanced" Second World countries share many of the same characteristics, and dissenters in both capitalist and socialist countries are awakening to this reality.

The concept of the overdeveloped society was first discussed in a book on *The Last Revolution* by the French development ethicist, L. J. Lebret, who perceived it as a political-economic condition rooted in cultural pathology. The overdeveloped society is similar to what Amitai Etzioni described as the "inauthentic" society, or Herbert Marcuse as "one-dimensional" living, or Lewis Mumford as the "machine society."

In the overdeveloped society, values, art, politics, education succumb to the process of technological rationality and its primary form, the advertised commodity. The old used-furniture dealer in Arthur Miller's *The Price* understands overdevelopment. "Today, the key word is disposable. The more you can throw away, the more it's beautiful. Your wife, children. The main thing today is shopping. Years ago, a man didn't know what to do with himself, he'd go to church, start a revolution. Today what do they do? Go shopping. If they would close the stores in this country for six months, there'd be a regular massacre."

The overdeveloped society has attempted to conquer both individual and institutional expressions of transcendence and morality. It resists any independent, empowering faith or critical moral action. "The result is the atrophy of the mental organs for grasping the contradictions and the alternatives and, in the one remaining dimension of technological rationality, the Happy Consciousness comes to prevail. It reflects the belief that the real is rational, and that the established system, in spite of everything, delivers the goods. The people are led to find in the productive apparatus the effective agent of thought and action to which their personal thought and action must be surrendered. And in this transfer, the apparatus also assumes the role of a moral agent."[12]

Not that there is a complete absence of opposition. Far from it. The over/under developed society is an experienced reality to a growing number of ethically alert persons to whom it means diminished existence. They understand that this society is in unstable crisis, fermenting, ready to change for better or worse.

The alternative to an overdeveloped society is *integral development*, wherein socioeconomic and political structures are changed to enhance the implementation of essential human values that one social theorist suggests are:

1. Multidimensional existence (versus the unidimen-

sional pattern of capitalist and socialist societies).

2. Community spirit guided by an ethic of solidarity (versus the rampant individualism of capitalist societies and the grim collectivism of socialist societies).

3. Work for human benefit (versus work for the benefit of the corporation or state).

4. Reduced consumption oriented toward being more (versus having more), and toward the growth of authentic community.

5. Liberating pedagogy and intergenerational dialogue oriented to the construction of the open, teaching-learning society (versus education to preserve the established system).

6. Tendencies toward egalitarian income distribution (versus widening class disparities).

7. Participation of all sectors of society (versus elite control and marginal masses).

8. Subordination of economic growth to integral development (versus subservience to economic growth per se).

9. Limitation of sovereignty by practical implementation of cooperation and solidarity at world and regional levels (versus unlimited sovereignty).

10. Integration with other national societies to enhance peace, economic welfare, and social justice (versus ideological, political, and economic isolation or conquest).[13]

An Overdeveloped Church

The church shares in the pathology of over/under development by relating to the socioeconomic order like the company town relates to its dominating enterprise. The overdeveloped church exhibits characteristics that are strikingly parallel to those of the overdeveloped society itself. It is:

—uncritical of capital- and energy-intensive technological "progress."

—insulated from and hostile to the needs of poor, powerless people.

—oblivious to and uncaring of the natural habitat.

—conspicuous in its consumption and expenditures for self-maintenance.

—led by officers who are disproportionately powerful and wealthy.

—oriented to personal therapy and charity rather than to social justice.

—managed by inappropriate organizational technology.

There are important exceptions to these generalizations about the behavior of the overdeveloped church. In many congregations there are members and officers who have covenanted to change their life-style in the direction of justice, stewardship, and community. They want to be part of the movement to live "abundantly," to share resources with the liberality that befits God's liberating grace, and to participate in social change for the common good. They see a clear distinction between "liberative action based on personal conviction" and being members of "consumer majorities who are artificially bound to Christianity."[14]

Having evaluated our situation and named our social condition, how shall we respond? What contribution should and can the Christian community make to life beyond the over/under developed society? The condition of overdevelopment, of course, is unstable. It will change *either* through a participatory politics that redefines abundance and distributes power and resources more fairly, *or* the overdeveloped society will lurch through a series of severe economic and political crises that no management by elites can handle humanely.

Cognitively and emotionally, Christians know that God is making all things new, reforming and reconciling the whole creation. The horizon of the future is always open, presenting both threat and promise, chaos and order, inhumanity and justice. In this perspective, God has created a universe that is far more dynamic, intricate, and changeable than human beings can fathom. (Christian faith is no more deterministic than is contemporary physics.) The future, like the universe itself, emerges from the questions we ask, the observations we make, the intentionality we project.

Christian thought expects no tidy extrapolation of present social trends, either positive or negative, but a growth of wheat and tares together until the harvest (Matt. 13:24–30). Reinhold Niebuhr suggested that the growth of evil with good was necessary because they could not always be distinguished. He did not address the problem that both might be magnified in a crowded world, making ethical choices ever more significant. Neither righteousness nor sin has a bit part in the scenario of Christian hope!

QUALITIES OF FAITHFULNESS

Reflecting on the German church struggle during the Nazi era, Helmut Gollwitzer concluded, "The way must always lead from the center to the periphery; reflection on this center is thus the most relevant and promising of all undertaking in unsettled times."

Amid a deepening social crisis, what are the marks of integrity or wholeness? What does it mean to be faithful Christians in our time? Faithfulness becomes possible "in Christ," the One who embodies human solidarity and breaks the bond of sin, freeing believers to be responsible, creative people (II Cor. 5:14–15) who can "distinguish between spirits" (I Cor. 12:10) and be "stewards of Christ and of the mysteries of God" (I Cor. 4:1). As the church's eyes are opened to the presence of God within the realities of a suffering world, Christians grasp what it means to live with integrity. Finding this treasure but covering it quickly and selling everything to purchase it, Christian ethics concentrates on the facets of faithful freedom.

Focal points of active faith or ethical dimensions of Christian faithfulness today encompass:

Qualities of Faithfulness	Corresponding Social Values
Hope in God's future	Liberation
Justice for the poor and oppressed	Sufficiency
Love of near and distant neighbors	Solidarity
Care for nature	Sustainability
Responsible use of power	Peace
Participation in community	Abundance

These interrelated qualities of faithfulness are a basic value framework[15] for whole Christian ministry. Each dimension of faithful action has Christological basis and secular implications here stated in terms of corresponding social values that provisionally embody the ethic of God's commonwealth.

Merely to list, even before explaining, qualities of *faithfulness* is to see that the over/under developed society, and each of us who inhabits it, adheres to other values: technocratic enthusiasm, cruel uprightness, grudging compassion, wasteful materialism, lust for power at the expense of other beings, self-serving religion and politics. To some degree the qualities of faithfulness elude every social system, group, and person. Our inclination toward faithlessness overwhelms our capacity for wholeness. Yet by no means does our "faithlessness nullify the faithfulness of God" (Rom. 3:3), or limit God's empowering grace.

A focus on *qualities* of faithfulness is especially appropriate in situations where many persons say, "Lord, Lord," but few do his teachings, and some want to express these values but are repelled by the behavior of existing churches. In a time when believing, doing, and belonging have become strangers to each other, wholeness must emerge from worldly efforts to exhibit these qualities. That, of course, is very much in the pattern of Jesus' ministry.

The function of the church is to say and do what communicates qualities of faithfulness. These are qualities of a faithful *church*, as well as believing individuals. A congregational and denominational life-style that exhibits some costly implications equips members for ministry and edifies the church (Eph. 4:12) even as it helps the world to comprehend the One in whom faithfulness originates.

Hope in God's Future

The church is called to new obedience to the reconciling-liberating God—the one whose name (Yahweh) means "I am who I will be," and "Let my people go!" Reconciliation is the clarifying event and historic goal of God's activity; liberation is the process for achieving it. Living between Christ's resurrection and return, believers are empowered—spirited enough—to engage the world and to stand up to death by embodying in provisional ways the New Jerusalem.

Hope based on God's action in Jesus Christ is the source of true freedom. All other hopes are illusory or subject to the crushing impact of political, economic, and natural events.

Because the resurrection is so hope-full, history becomes a theater of transformation. History acquires a missionary structure. The world becomes a laboratory of possible salvation—fermenting with future.

A fascinating consequence of Christian hope is that the church does not need to rely on the present order, nor defend existing arrangements of power and institutions. It no longer accepts as sacrosanct the myths by which society operates. To borrow a term from Thomas Merton, those who share Christian hope will be *disillusioned* about the idolized values, such as "rapid growth" or continuous "progress," or "peace through strength." A hopeful church abandons the religion of pattern-maintenance in favor of prophetic goal-attainment. Because it has no permanent abode in any existing social setting, the church is free to go "outside the camp" (Heb. 13:13), expecting to bear abuse as it suffers with and for others in search of the abundant life. Christian hope knows that God is doing a new thing, and that the church moves from what is to what will be in solidarity with the powerless.

Christian hope speaks to everyone's sense of powerlessness to change the system (subjectively, we are all proletarians). Faithful hope overcomes the prevailing sense of fate. It gives a vision to people who were nobodies and empowers them to act humanely in the face of oppressive policies and institutionalized violence.

Justice for the Poor and Oppressed

Theology begins from below and turns "the world upside down" (Acts 17:6). "The view from below" is a phrase Dietrich Bonhoeffer used in one of his letters from prison, before being executed for participating in the resistance against Hitler. Though he came from a secure, bourgeois background, Bonhoeffer engaged in acts of identification, caring, and risk, whereby he learned "to see the great events of world history from below, from the perspective of the outcast, the suspects, the maltreated, the powerless, the oppressed, the reviled—in short, from the perspective of those who suffer."[16] Ministry with this perspective expects God to scatter the proud and sides with those who lack right and privilege; it fills the hungry with good things but sends the rich empty away (Luke 1:51–53). Blessed are those who are persecuted for justice' sake, for theirs is the Kingdom.

The generous justice which the Bible teaches is not qualitatively different from the love God displays and demands. The love-justice unity is evident in the Gospels and Epistles which reassert the church's vocation to side with the poor. Jesus explains the great commandment (Luke 10:25ff.) in terms of compassion toward victims of injustice. "Love your neighbor as yourself [or as your own kin]" comes from Lev. 19:18, where it synthesizes and summarizes rules of just relations with aliens, orphans, widows, slaves, etc. (Cf. Deut. 15:8–15 and Jer. 22:15–16.)

In Jesus Christ is the decisive clue to the justice or righteousness (*dikaiosyne*) of God. In Christ we experience complete love, despite our unworthiness, and are enabled to be whole.

"One of the powers the justified 'enjoy' is the power to 'do' justice in such wise that their actions are intrinsically linked to God's actions in redeeming and reordering the world. Just as Jesus' death and resurrection have brought us the power which we did not deserve, so that acquittal has won for us the power which we have not merited. That power is nothing less than God's own justice enabling us to perform actions which no human capacities would be competent to perform. . . . Insofar as human beings are rooted in the justice of God, so the justice of God can be enfleshed in human actions and human institutions."[17] Our efforts can only approximate God's loving justice. To expect more invites despair; to expect less invites inaction.

The natural temptation of middle-class Christians in every society is to spiritualize the announcement of liberation and to cut it loose from a rigorous social analysis. This pitfall is avoided when we participate in transforming action that

—Starts with the suffering of the poor or marginalized and seeks to change the way things are.
—Attends to "nonpersons" (the powerless and victimized) who ask, "How can we believe in God in a society that systematically crushes and destroys us?"
—Uses the tools of social science to analyze patterns of power, dependency, and conflict between oppressors and oppressed in particular social settings.
—Issues from, and leads to, engagement (ortho-praxis), which fosters an integration of right doing and right thinking.[18]

Particularly the overdeveloped church that has learned to be at ease in a material Zion must relearn how to change life-style in ways that serve justice and live abundantly with limited resources and reduced economic growth. These are primary personal and political goals for Christian worship, nurture, and witness today.

Sufficiency is the *norm* of justice in our time. "The world quite literally can no longer afford the injustices and the excesses of the rich. It can no longer afford the production/consumption patterns of middle-class America. Despite the larger populations of the poor countries, it is we who are most implicated in depleting the resources and upsetting the stability of the ecosystems, and grasping too much of everything that everybody needs. And if the limits to economic growth are at last to be taken seriously, there can be no cheap justice through the spreading or trickling of our kind of prosperity to all. The extreme maldistribution of wealth is an obstacle that will have to be removed if the world is to have a just and sustainable future."[19]

Sufficiency is the *flexible* norm of justice. It does not specify rigidly what is sufficient for all everywhere. It takes into account various kinds of insufficiency, and emphasizes that ideas of sufficiency must be tested ecumenically in the light of the principle that "some minimal sufficiency for everyone takes precedence ... over anyone's right to enjoy a surplus.... A generally accepted norm of sufficiency would radically change the life-style of most Americans! It would focus our attention on insufficiency among the poor and the real meaning of abundance for those who have goods but lack the good life."[20]

Sufficiency is the *direction* for life-style change and political action; it is a creative norm that does not set exact specifications for everyone to follow. But it does assume a choice between God and wealth. The just posture is to seek sufficiency of goods and services for all, as in the petition, "Give us our daily bread." No one can live by bread alone, or without bread. "But to ask for bread for today does not mean wanting bread for always, even beyond death, nor more bread than is necessary, especially when the accumulation of this wealth often implies that others go without their daily bread."[21] Sufficiency means an economics of equality in which we gather according to what we can eat (Ex. 16:17), and share our abundance to supply others' want (II Cor. 8:13–14).

Love of Near and Distant Neighbors

First John reminds us that faithfulness to the God, who loves us despite our unworthiness, is expressed in loving relations with neighbors, however "worthy" or "deserving." First Thessalonians contains a petition that love may increase and overflow toward one another and toward all (I Thess. 3:12) *All* on this planet includes the whole inhabited world and unborn generations.

The moment God "gets through" to us with a love that accepts, judges, and liberates, we are impelled to share it fully with others. Justice is love distributed to all, through social policies and institutional structures. Love gives clear direction and character to justice, in the light of Jesus' deeds and teachings.

Jesus both radicalized the meaning and expanded the scope of love. Radicalized love involves simplicity, sharing, and suffering. Expanded love of neighbor breaks through the barriers of culture, religion, race, sex, and nation—to express mutual humanity.

Christian love, in short, is socially revolutionary. The neighbor love that Jesus taught and practiced dissolved the traditional bond between sin and poverty, between virtue and success. "Blessed are you poor, for yours is the Kingdom of God." "How hard it will be for those who have riches to enter the Kingdom of God."

The life of love takes the *form* of solidarity with the exploited, a love of justice for them. Solidarity aptly characterizes how human beings can show the love of

God—God's solidarity with humanity—to others. Just as sufficiency is the norm of justice, solidarity is a form of love.

The capacity of the church to be in solidarity with the world is not self-derived. It is a gift of koinonia, the community-creating Spirit, in whose bond persons and groups become *les animateurs du solidarité*, "creators of solidarity."

Solidarity behavior demonstrates that "we are all in the same boat." If justice means the common good, solidarity means unity and mutuality as human beings. A witness to solidarity particularly affirms human equality and advocates human rights.

Twentieth-century Christian ethics has frequently affirmed the equal worth of human beings in God's creation. This theme has characterized Public Christianity since the days of social Darwinism. Yet the issue is still with us in policy proposals that would deliberately neglect segments of society or the human race for the sake of "survival."

Without factual warrant, survival utilitarianism permits the suffering or sacrifice of X numbers and groups of people in order to relieve the pressure on resources. Survival thinking unethically ignores the causes of current misery as well as the combination of policy changes that would diminish hunger and poverty. Moreover, it contradicts Christian ethical spontaneity and the obligation to assess and respond to immediate human need. It contradicts the biblical teaching that all, rich and poor, are created in the image of God and are loved equally by the Creator, who has special compassion for the least. Faithful people know that the fundamental planetary reality consists *not* of lifeboats, basket cases, and trade-offs, but of the recognition that we share mutual human dignity or degradation.

Advocates of solidarity witness to human dignity; identify with resistance against repression; join the quest for self-government, freedom of movement, liberty to read, hear and express ideas; form associations and organize for political action. Solidarity ethics is interested in human rights from the viewpoint of both civil rights and social rights, a matter on which Third World liberation theologies could have been clearer. Feminist theology is very clear about the connection.

> In our present world the rising expectation of many oppressed peoples has led them to participate in their own movements toward liberation. Women belong to one of the groups who find that the liberties gained have not been adequate. As an oppressed majority they seek to break the peculiar chains of sexism which bind us all, both women and men. Aware of their solidarity with others in groaning, they want to add their own contribution to the revolutions of freedom. . . . They have joined the procession of their sisters in every age, in demanding freedom *from* dehumanizing social structures, in order that they might become free *for* participation in the social, political, and economic struggles for humanization which are taking place in our global society.[22]

Wherever it occurs, repression of basic human rights (including civil liberties) ought to be challenged by acts of solidarity, beginning with publicity of the facts, telling the stories of the victims, and interceding in their behalf through politics as well as prayer. In a setting of political liberty, acts of solidarity include both intercession and intervention, both local involvement and global witness. Special concern needs to be expressed for the rights of near neighbors (e.g., in the local criminal justice system or of the unemployed) as well as the elementary rights of distant persons and groups.

Care for Nature

The community that seeks social justice will join the quest for environmental renewal. Human well-being depends on both, together. In fact, the biblical prophets knew instinctively that where justice is done, nature also thrives; where injustice thrives, the land becomes barren. Within an interconnected creation, all are neighbors. All includes past, present, and future generations of human beings as well as the natural habitat.

The community of faith shares responsibility for human well-being communally, ecologically, and intergenerationally. Motivation to care for the habitat stems from faith in the providence of God who has purposes that include unborn generations (Gen. 12:15; 28:13–14; Ex. 33:1). Inheritors of a good land must preserve and enhance it as a trust for future generations (cf. Deut. 6:10–11). This is the ecological significance of the communion of saints. Humans exist in nature, and both are vulnerable to sin. Biblical wisdom recognizes that what people do and how nature acts are closely interrelated. "Is it not enough for you to feed on the good pastures, . . . and to drink of clear water, that you must foul the rest with your feet?" (Ezek. 34:18) Violence toward people violates nature, and vice versa. The practice of injustice leads to social chaos and a barren environment.

> (Injustice) There is swearing, lying, killing, stealing, and committing adultery.

> (Chaos) Therefore the land mourns, and all who dwell in it languish, and also the beasts of the field, and the birds of the air; and even the fish of the sea. (Hos. 4:2–3)

> (Injustice) Hear this, you heads of the house of Jacob . . . who abhor justice and pervert all equity, who build Zion with blood and Jerusalem with wrong.

> (Chaos) Zion shall be plowed as a field; Jerusalem shall become a heap of ruins, and the mountain of the house a wooded height. (Micah 3:9–12)

Nature shares the catastrophe prophesied by Jeremiah. His picture of the desolate land suggests the aftermath of a nuclear explosion (Jer. 4:23–26).

These prophetic warnings, and their positive counterpart in the eschatological visions, clearly show that justice to the poor and care for nature are two sides of the same coin. They are twin foci in an ethic of *eco-justice*.[23] The ethic of eco-justice defines a caretaking form of human dominion over plants and animals, and equitable steward-ship of the oikos—the habitat and all its inhabitants. The steward in Luke 12:41ff. is accountable for faithful deal-ings, not primarily for profits earned.

On this side of Rachel Carson's *Silent Spring*, Barry Commoner's *The Closing Circle*, and several years of theological-ethical reflection on the prospect of ecological catastrophe, the ecumenical church has begun to consider the requirements for a just, participatory, and *sustainable* society. The norm of sustainable harmony finally received equal time in the late 1970s, particularly in the 1979 World Conference on Faith, Science, and the Future, convened by the World Council of Churches at Cambridge, Massa-chusetts. Australian biologist, Charles Birch, who chaired the gathering, noted that a common conceptual environ-ment, rather than the fruits of science and technology per se, will determine the future of humanity. Scientific inqui-ry must abandon the mechanistic image of nature and humanity and, instead, affirm the unity or oneness of nature, humanity, and God. The community of faith can foster a new life ethic which embraces and is accountable to humanity and nature together. Only on such a founda-tion will we build an ecologically sustainable and socially just society.[24]

At the same conference, economist Herman Daly from Louisiana warned of the ecological necessity to limit economic growth, given the threat to *renewable* resources of forests, fisheries, grasslands, croplands, and water re-sources. A sustainable economy requires a protected re-newable resource base and a scale of population and per capita consumption that is within the sustainable yield of the renewable resource base. Modern growth economics is like Promethean paganism in its devotion to increasing the total throughput with no recognition of the limited biophysical budget. Over against this exploitation of the future, Daly offers the following general rule of right action: *"sufficient per capita product for the greatest number over time."*[25]

"Number over time" is accountable to future life and subhuman life as well as present human beings. The general rule of right action retains the economist's substitution of goods for The Good in the interest of operationality, but the rule applies to goods the condition of "sufficient" rather than "greatest" (in contrast to Jeremy Bentham's utilitarian rule of "the greatest good for the greatest number"). Since production is not The Good, it should not be maximized. Production is a good thing up to a point of sufficient production, after which it detracts from the good. By substituting "sufficient" for "greatest" the rule avoids the logical fallacy of having one too many "greatests." The maximization of numbers is subject to the prior constraint of sufficient per capita product. Sufficient for what? Sufficient for a good life. "Greatest number over time" requires that the population of each generation be limited to the carrying capacity. This extends the commandment, "Thou shalt not kill" to include, "Thou shalt not destroy the capacity of creation to support life." To destroy carrying capacity in pursuit of maximum production is a sign of idolatry, not stewardship.

An eco-justice ethic highlights the *wisdom* of the organic, the gentle, the nonviolent, the elegant and beautiful, and the smaller. "Ever-bigger machines, entailing ever-bigger concentrations of economic power and exerting ever-greater violence against the environment, do not represent progress; they are a denial of wisdom," warned E. F. Schumacher. Wisdom demands the opposite orientation translated into methods and equipment which are *cheap* enough to be accessible to virtually everyone, *suitable* for small-scale application, and *compatible* with the human need for creativity. "Out of these three characteristics is born non-violence and a relationship of human beings to nature which guarantees permanence. If any of these three is neglected, things are bound to go wrong."[26]

Conventional wisdom has held that large size is good because it produces economies of scale that are reputed to be more efficient, and because economic concentration is deemed necessary for material advance. But this ideology says little about the common social good, care for persons, continuity of communities, or the fragile ecology. Smallerness puts a premium on human scale—renewable resources, decentralized technology, social stewardship, and careful responses to imbalanced ecosystems—for the sake of a sustainable human society.

Responsible Use of Power

The ecumenical body of Christ is empowered to act for a better future in the light of the kingdom ethic, or the vision of shalom. "Organizationally speaking, the churches are a global network capable of combining information with moral education, finance and programmatic action in a way not easy to duplicate. One becomes especially conscious of this capacity in some developing countries where the government and the church are literally the only national networks, and of the two the church is the older and sometimes more extensive system with impressive grass-roots strength. All the social changes needed to remedy [poverty and injustice] call for *social* action; and, in the simplest sociological sense, the church already is a social action—'one body with many members.' "[27]

A faithful church makes a witness that challenges idolatry and expresses the new vision in society. The people of the new covenant are moved with inward energy toward outward action, showing that peace is on its way for all because it is already being lived among them.

The overdeveloped society characteristically idolizes violent energy systems and military force. Idolatry of violent power assumes that the mighty will inherit the earth. The dual irony of this power-idolizing policy is that it undermines the general social welfare in the name of security, and it threatens humane survival by the way it defends freedom. Increased military production and use of military force deepens poverty, accelerates unemployment, intensifies urban and rural community deterioration, and violates human rights while keeping unjust order.

Here, again, more means worse. The more military defense, the less social security and development; the more planned nuclear dismemberment of human beings, the less likely we are to avoid cataclysm. Nuclear terrorism threatens to sacrifice whole cities and nations as the superpowers develop "counter-force" weapons. In the new phase of the arms race, let us pray that the electronic monitors do not see missiles where there is a flock of geese![28]

Christians have a vision of a city where people dwell together in peace because there is justice. Toward that end Christians must struggle against idolatry of the death machine which many citizens and officials view as a source of saving power. In the Bible there is a striking mythological image for this death machine. It is the image of Leviathan, the multiheaded monster which ascends from the murky depths to spread chaos. "Terror dances before him" (Job 41:22). Nothing seems to stop it, and who can fight against it? The whole earth is awed and worships the beast. And those who worship Leviathan will be slain by it (Rev. 13:15). Instead of bowing the knee to the death machine, Christians are called to witness to the Prince of Peace, who finally subjects brute military power to the power of nonviolence.[29]

Christians have the freedom and capacity to refuse to support systems of violence that spawn nuclear weapons, arms sales, and economic injustice. Instead of being defensive, Christians can comprehend the structured violence (both overt and covert) that dominates society, and Christians can embody costly nonviolent love in situations of oppression.

The ecumenical Christian community recognizes that the violence of the powerful from above spawns the violent opposition of the powerless from below. While this produces a double inhuman effect, there is a moral difference between managing oppression and resisting it. Regimes and structures that squash movements for justice within the system and liquidate protestors (even the nonviolent) must be replaced or overthrown, preferably through nonviolent resistance. But it may mean Christian participation in violent acts of liberation or tyrannicide as a last resort, when all else fails, in particular moments. A responsible use of power is governed, therefore, by a principle of "selective conscientious objection to violence."[30]

Now we begin to discern the full power of Christians—power to relinquish, share, and exercise. Few readers of these words are actually in controlling positions to decide the direction of agencies, companies, or organizations. But most of us have influence in particular settings. And typically, we are in an ambiguous both-and relation to oppressors and oppressed. We benefit from various forms of oppression while we are in some ways victimized, along with persons and groups who are more oppressed. We have numerous choices as to our support of both in our daily work and the policies we advocate.

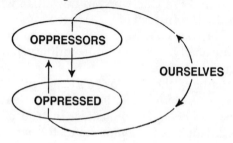

Participation in Community

The ecumenical benefits of Christ are that he brings the far off near, breaks down every dividing wall of hostility, and creates a new humanity of persons who are no longer strangers or sojourners but fellow citizens of one *oikos*, "public household" (Eph. 2:11–22). Here, economic responsibility and ecumenical relations are of a piece.

Many Christians hunger for, but few regularly experience, this biblically promised community, let alone its social correlates. The church organizations most of us know conform to the world much more than they help to transform human relationships. We hunger for deep associations of persons with whom we can be ourselves, share dreams and hopes, and count on creative support in implementing faithful aspirations.

If such community is elusive among believers, it is even harder to find in the secular structures of the overdeveloped society. The American ethos especially lacks genuinely communal bonds based on a covenantal sense of equality among plural races and mutual caring for the poor and the land. "Like the high-flying mythic figure of Icarus, whose too high ascent toward the sun resulted in disaster as the wax that bound the feathers in his wings melted, [we are oblivious] to the disaster that comes from overlooking the finite realities of our interrelatedness. . . . Only a sense of the covenant with land and humanity that implies reciprocal caring could keep our finitude before us so as to counter our invincible innocence. In other words, only an *alteration* of the myth can open Americans to the covenantal realities of our common life."[31]

Why does the overdeveloped society experience such a deterioration of basic community services—education, health care, cooperative food production and marketing, decent housing, public security, sufficient public transportation, emergency assistance, and income maintenance? And why are so many Christians willing to cut public funding of human services? No doubt, this is due in part to populist hostility toward government bureaucracy, in part to a prevailing voluntarist ideology that favors private over public programs, and in part to anxiety over reduced personal affluence which fuels the movement to reduce taxes—any taxes. The cause underlying these symptoms, however, is *alienation* from community. In their quest for self-esteem and well-being, people substitute consumption for community. "But the overconsumptive style of life is a phony way to meet such needs. Material success and the abundance of possessions do not really measure our worth as human beings. The status that we think we get from conformity to the established patterns of affluence is a poor substitute indeed for the affirmation of ourselves that would come in authentic relationships with our fellow human beings."[32]

"I came that you may have life, and have it abundantly" (John 10:10). The abundance to which Jesus points is found in the nurture and enjoyment of restored relationships. We can take the crucial step of entering a faithful community of support—a church within the church—that affirms changes of life-style consistent with the qualities of faithfulness outlined above.

A faithful community of support is necessary because, as Martin Buber observed, "We live by communion as well as bread." By the grace of God and with help from our friends we are transformed, though slowly. Gradually we learn what the African means in saying, "I am, because I participate." The secret of community is beyond our capability to structure at will. It occurs in moments and movements of koinonia or communitas, when we experience a social embodiment of God's grace or a quality of relationship between persons which is radically open to the transcendent Kingdom. The essence of community is given to us; "What we are [given] together is what we shall be for others."[33] We are given the bond of the Spirit which enables us to live faithfully.

Part II / MODES OF MINISTRY

Introduction to Part II

Every act of a minister who would be prophetic is part of a way of evoking, forming, and reforming an alternative community. And this applies to every facet and every practice of ministry. It is a measure of our enculturation that the various acts of ministry (for example, counseling, administration, even liturgy) have taken on lives and functions of their own rather than being seen as elements of the one prophetic ministry of formation and reformation of alternative community.
—Walter Brueggemann, *The Prophetic Imagination*

The ministry of the church *is* social ministry; social ministry involves all the functions of the church. The following chapters are designed to rediscover the social or public significance of all forms of regular ministry, and to perceive the one ministry that occurs through each of these modes, and the whole ministry that occurs through action that interrelates the modes.

The modes of ministry explored in the next six chapters divide into two groups as indicated in the listing below:

CHAPTERS 4–7	CHAPTERS 8–9
Liturgy (Public Prayer)	Social Service—Advocacy
Preaching (Biblical Interpretation)	Community Organization— Development
Education Fostered by the Church	Public Policy Action
Pastoral Care and Counseling	Institutional Governance— Corporate Responsibility
Empowering Lay Ministry	

The first group of modes has seldom been perceived as social ministry. The second group has seldom been developed in regular congregational ministry.

The first set of modes needs to be resocialized beyond the private and psychological dimensions that have so preoccupied parish ministers. The second set of modes can be reappropriated as "real stuff" for parish ministry along with the first set, and not merely as options for those congregations which have the time or inclination. The modes in the second set have become rather routinized and impersonal (mechanical), perhaps because they have been relegated to extra-parish settings for the most part. So there is a special need to clarify the fresh focus and to personalize the congregation's involvement in the second set of modes of ministry, even as we consider how to resocialize the first set.

Keep in mind that these are modes of *congregational* ministry, not ways professionals serve clients, or shepherds attend sheep already in the fold. They involve the mutual ministry of believers serving others and acting for justice in a suffering world. In each mode it is essential to develop a people's ministry in society beyond the routine pattern wherein pastors serve parishioners.

I did not invent these modes, though I have relabeled and clarified some of them. The modes have a long history in the life of the church, and are represented in the work of congregations today. But few congregations as yet encompass these modes comprehensively and dynamically.

In exploring each mode of ministry, consider: What is its theological-social purpose? Identify the most urgent problem(s) in developing this mode. What characteristic temptation or pitfall confronts our efforts? What alternative insight(s) may refresh this ministry? What specifically are we trying to do more effectively? Which skills do we need to learn/teach? Which methods and models are available to us? How does this mode fit into an overall strategy of ministry?

These questions provide a framework for individual note-taking and an agenda for continuing education that develops the congregation's competence in all of these modes of ministry. Precisely as congregations and regional church bodies acquire these competencies, and develop the gifts of individuals and groups to use them, will they engage in whole ministry.

4

Social Dimensions of Liturgy

Formal worship is liturgy, preachers are liturgists, the members of the body of Christ are liturgists in their "worshipping," in their care for each other, and in their work in the world, and Christ is *the* liturgist.
— Floyd D. Shafer, *Liturgy: Worship and Work*

For Jesus, all cultic demands must be subservient to human need, whether physical or spiritual, and to interpersonal reconciliation.
— Massey H. Shepherd, Jr., *Liturgy and Education*

The most regular occasion for social ministry occurs in public worship, a weekly battleground with "the principalities and powers." There the worshiping community encounters the transcendent mystery of God, who radically loves the world while suffering with its meek inhabitants, heals human ills by enduring and breaking the chains of oppression, and sets people right through costly acts of justice. Yet many gatherings for worship seem to forget the out-of-bondage-bringing God in their search for a Tolerant Friend and Handy Fixer, and many liturgists refer infrequently to public events in their preoccupation with accumulated personal hurts.

Much worship fails to pull us out of self-concern into the orbit of God's gracious power, to share the values of the transforming Commonwealth through prayers, hymns, proclamation, sacrament, and symbolic action, and to confront the crisis that we benefit from unjust patterns and live idolatrously. "We have sought safety rather than justice. We have profited from making arms rather than sacrificing for peace, and have not beaten our swords into plowshares. We have called arrogance patriotism and made a god of our race. We have indulged our greed, ignored the poor, and misused the land. We have cursed our enemies and exploited our families and friends. Forgive us, Lord, and send your Spirit now to heal the brokenness of our lives."[1]

Worship (along with the rest of congregational life) should help us fulfill our baptismal vow to "renounce the bondage of sin and the injustices of this world" and to "accept the liberty which God gives." The complicated question is just how to do this in theologically disciplined ways that steer clear of quietism on the one hand and fanaticism on the other.

I recall a decade ago discussing with my father, a student of Karl Barth and a signer of the Theological Declaration of Barmen, what ought to be emphasized in the liturgy. We disagreed about the social role of the church. He was uneasy with activist motifs. I was looking for more than cheap grace. Our difference was not in depth of conviction. I could feel his emotion whenever we sang Luther's "Ein' feste Burg," the protest hymn of the Barmen Confessors. The Theological Declaration of Barmen was a crucial defense of the gospel in resistance to the Nazi regime's overt incursion into doctrinal teaching and church governance. But because that state-supported church had a venerable tradition of sociopolitical silence, it reacted only belatedly to the ethical issue of anti-Semitism, and it challenged only indirectly the totalitarian regime.

North American Protestants in the ecumenical denominations share a livelier tradition of ethics informed by the Social Gospel tradition. But an easygoing theological pluralism may make us just as vulnerable to severe collective pathology and no more prepared to make a confessional witness as the American crisis deepens. This underscores an urgent need to develop public worship that fosters faithful social witness.

Liturgy, like education, either domesticates or liberates. There is no middle ground. Domesticating liturgy justifies the way things are; it encourages people to acquiesce to dominant social norms as did the German Christians under Nazi domination, the moderate American churches during recent social movements, and today's popular right-wing preachers who invoke God's name in defense of national power and conventional mores.

A liberating liturgy on the other hand empowers groups of believers to comprehend the sufferings of God and to develop alternative (prophetic) praxis, as did the Confessing Church under Hitler, and the ecumenical movements for civil rights, peace, women's equality, human rights, and as does the cosmopolitan church that takes shape around liberation theologies. Each of those movements has produced liturgical experiences with deep commitment to and active unity in the liberating-reconciling themes of Scripture. In such action, we present our "bodies as a living sacrifice, holy and acceptable to God, which is [our] spiritual worship" (Rom. 12:1). Those who have participated in socially alert *leitourgia* can only be impatient with domesticating forms of worship.

Liturgy, of course, is creative work; the root meaning of the term is the people's work in the light of God's work. It is what God says and does to and through the church. The word *leitourgia* is used in the New Testament to refer to common worship (Acts 13:2), to the work of liturgists or ministers (Rom. 15:16), to the service of the poor (Rom. 15:27) and of fellow members (Phil. 2:25, 30), as well as to the ministry of Christ (Heb. 8:6).

Dietrich Bonhoeffer proposed that "our being Christian today will be limited to two things: prayer and doing justice. All Christian thinking, speaking, and organizing must be born anew out of this prayer and action."[2] His was a fresh portrayal of love of God and neighbor. He noted that corporate worship and Bible study develop the inner discipline and purposeful confidence to act outwardly for just social policies. "The two elements must stand in dialectic with one another. Of itself, without 'doing justice,' the hidden discipline would revive the worst of the sectarian style. The close Christian community would become the pious and self-righteous ghetto . . . a 'fossil church.' . . . At the same time, and without 'prayer,' doing justice by itself would soon result in Christianity as a burn-out case, dying with the particular causes with which it was identified in a passing age . . . a 'chameleon church.' . . . Left to itself the hidden discipline would become but another form of spiritual tribalism; and doing justice, by itself, just another round of exhausting partisan involvement. But in dialectic, the hidden discipline provides the sustaining power for the long-term engagement for the common good. . . . And doing justice supplies much of the setting, means, and materials for discovering 'who Christ really is, for us today.' "[3]

In liturgy the faithful community unites symbolic and social action. Liturgy is the life-style of the community which gathers for prayer, praise, fellowship, and ministry in the world. If worship is to undergird that life-style, then leaders must be alert to the whole liturgical environment. Which behavior of God is being praised by what means? What pattern of thanksgiving, confession, petition, intercession, and celebration are we elicting? How do we encompass public concerns and private fears? To what structured opportunities for mission/ministry does our worship point?

There are many nuances to this evaluation of our liturgy's social character. Here I stress three dimensions of socially healthy liturgy: knowledge of God, public prayer, and shared ministry.

Knowledge of God

Starting with God's liturgy, we can set aside the myth that a resocialized liturgy is merely a liberal or radical political agenda imposed on the design of worship. In fact, one of the common failings of contemporary worship across the conservative-liberal spectrum is its anthropocentrism. Too frequently worship highlights our salvation status or our psychological well-being, or our programmatic activity. The mighty acts of God are assumed or ignored. "The coming together of people and their formation into an interdependent community must be understood as always initiated and accomplished by God. Only by God's Word and Act are they made into a 'royal priesthood' and 'God's own people.' (I Peter 2:9) Yet one often receives the impression that the people themselves create this community by what they do with and for one another, if not with and for God, so that the liturgy is turned into a kind of celebration of 'togetherness.' "[4] At the center of the liturgy is the radically social work of the triune God. Therefore, the way we speak of who God is and what God does in the world is crucial to vital liturgy—to God's continuing work in and through us.

Who is God? What God images are usually employed in our prayers, hymns, Sacraments, and rites of passage? To what extent do they express Hebraic unity of thought which avoids dualism of nature and supernature, sacred and secular, spiritual and worldly, transcendent and imminent? Less use (which is not to exclude use) of such images as Lord, King, and Sovereign Ruler is necessary not only to overcome sexism. It is necessary to avoid images of divine remoteness, social hierarchy, and political passivity. God who is "beyond and ahead," and "rising up" to bring people out of bondage need not be portrayed as "over and above," with arbitrary powers of life and death. The Creator, Redeemer, and Sanctifier "in and through" life is history's source, river, matrix, ground, way, servant, horizon, fount of wisdom, promised future. We have only begun to mine the rich language of Scripture to express God's transcendent, liberating, mysterious presence within and beyond history.

God's loving justice for the world in Jesus Christ can be

more effectively communicated by abandoning sexist imagery and recognizing God's inclusive character. God is Lord, Servant, King, and Shepherd, but also Wisdom, Spirit, Sustainer of Life, Heart's Delight, Woman in Travail, Binder of Wounds, Dresser of Nature, Searcher for a Lost Coin, Tender Forgiver, Compassionate Giver, Companion in Sorrow, Teacher of Peace. Use of this enriched imagery is a key element of social liturgy.

As inclusive imagery becomes a thoroughgoing practice in hymns, prayers, Sacraments, it moves the church to act accordingly. Such liturgical habit is an expression of justice toward the majority sex in both church and society, some of whose members have become increasingly restive if not alienated over the insensitivity of male leadership. No longer is it acceptable to conclude that it is unimportant or impossible to begin the Lord's Prayer, "Our Father and Mother. . . ." Resources are at hand to change God-language responsibly.[5]

What does God do? Our prayer should reflect a lively knowledge of what God is doing in the world, that is, the divine politics.

The biblical drama that sparks liturgical imagination has very political content. God creates the world, chooses a people, delivers them from slavery, makes covenant with them, gives them a land, and spells out a "law" that is administered by judges, violated by kings, and proclaimed by prophets. The people are exiled, but the dispersed remnant is promised a Messiah, the Servant who inaugurates the new age of the Kingdom of God. The new commonwealth is established through the public ministry of Jesus, whose love for the oppressed and nonviolent disruption of the established order leads to his death as a convict and his victory over the powers of the age as risen Lord. Followers of Jesus—people of the Way—are moved by the Spirit to proclaim liberty, to heal the sick, to develop a caring common life, and to challenge the principalities and powers—in order to establish right human relations. At the center of it all—the hinge to both Testaments—is the political activity of the crucified Messiah: Anointed One, Suffering Servant, Authoritative Teacher, Good Shepherd, Compassionate Healer, Doer of Wondrous Signs, Ruler of all principalities and powers.

The purpose of worship is to participate in this action of God and to engender faithful witness. Liturgy that focuses on what God is doing in the world will let socially potent biblical symbols, narratives, and poetry do their work in patterning perception, stimulating consciousness, and reorienting ministry.

Public Prayer

Thomas Merton, in *Seasons of Celebration*, asserted that "liturgy is, in the original and classical sense of the word, a political activity. *Leitourgia* was a 'public work,' a contribution made by a free citizen of the polis to the celebration and manifestation of the visible life of the *polis*." We are involved in public worship of God, not a private act. Public worship should have public concerns; its purpose is not to withdraw from but to move us into public life again. It reaffirms our common humanity, our unity beyond separateness, our linkage as strangers become friends by the grace of our Lord Jesus Christ. "True unity comes by discovering the One who brings us together, the One who is found in prayer, the One who lives in each of us and allows us to identify each other."[6]

The One who made friends with all humanity through a public ministry that led to a cross cannot be worshiped in a socially passive way. To focus on the cross as a worship symbol is to highlight an instrument of cruel execution set on a garbage dump outside a city wall. To remember him in Communion is to be directly involved with sociopolitical realities. The bread is broken; the wine is poured. As we partake of the broken bread and poured wine, we remember how that bread was broken and the wine was spilled. Thus we get in touch with the true mystery of

God's re-creating love, the reality of God's renewing power, and God's obvious (though not only) objective that bread be shared by everyone and injustice be done by no one.

This makes us critically conscious of the subject matter of prayer. Public prayer features gratitude and petition for God's liberating-reconciling action, while expressing anguish, frustration, and longing amid public events. As in the Psalms, a full range of feelings and meanings are pertinent to a prayerful relationship with the free, active God who infuses all of life. Authentic prayers of the people celebrate God's gift of shalom, rejoice in God's loving justice, express solidarity with victims of oppression, protest dangerous or wicked enterprises that cloak their deeds in the name of order, freedom, security, or justice, and anticipate God's power to intercede for the poor and meek.

Anyone who has sat through numerous pastoral prayers knows that most of them only obliquely and occasionally touch public concerns. Such prayers may include "concerns of the people" but overwhelmingly they concern individual illness and personal crisis. The prayers of the people in the public worship of God ought to focus on larger corporate concerns as a first priority, without excluding personal crises. Many of the traditional collects found in the better prayer books are at least corroborating evidence of the larger public purpose of common prayer.

The trouble with many of the traditional collects, however, is their tendency to foster rather uncritical obedience to civil authority. They reflect a liturgy that serves the social establishment. They stretch the meaning of Romans 13 while ignoring the implications of Revelation 13. They pray for the established holders of power, but not very often for those who deserve and are seeking people power. Nevertheless the liturgical tradition has explicit social content, which is more than can be said for some contemporary pastoral prayers.

Closely related to social domestication of Christian worship has been the privatizing of confession. All too often, prayers of confession screen out issues of social policy while focusing on personal-family relations. What kind of sin does your congregation habitually confess? Compare your congregation's prayer with the following litany.[7]

LEADER: Creator Spirit, you made the world and everything in it; you created the human race of one stock and gave us the earth for our possession.

PEOPLE: *Break down the walls that separate us and unite us in a single body.*

LEADER: Gracious God, we have been divisive in our thinking, in our speech, in our actions;
we have classified and imprisoned one another;
we have fenced each other out by hatred and prejudice.

PEOPLE: *Break down the walls that separate us and unite us in a single body.*

LEADER: Loving Reconcilor, you mean us to be a single people, ruled by peace, feasting in freedom, freed from injustice, truly human, men and women, responsible and responsive in the life we lead, the love we share, the relationships we create.

PEOPLE: *Break down the walls that separate us and unite us in a single body.*

LEADER: Source of all Truth, we shall need ever-new insights into the truth, awareness of your will for all humanity, courage to do what is right even when it is not allowed, persistence in undermining unjust structures until they crumble into dust, grace to exercise a ministry of reconciliation.

PEOPLE: *Break down the walls that separate us and unite us in a single body.*

LEADER: Power of Life, share out among us the tongues of your Spirit, that we may each burn with compassion for all who hunger for freedom and humanness; that we may be doers of the Word and so speak with credibility about the wonderful things you have done.

LEADER AND PEOPLE: *Lord, direct us in ways we do not yet discern and equip us for the service of reconciliation and liberation in your world.*

How does your liturgy render visible the hidden exploitation of the poor and powerless, or pinpoint the sins of the affluent and powerful? The church frequently focuses on the wrong kinds of sin. We have a "beam in our own eye," due to an overdose of Puritan perfectionism, revivalist individualism, class privilege, and the tendency to psychologize. Together these influences have caused us to neglect the "weightier matters of the law—justice and mercy and faith." Ezekiel, who repeatedly denounced ungodly behavior, reminded his hearers that the guilt of Sodom was that the people of that city "had pride, surfeit of food, and prosperous ease, but did not aid the poor and needy. They were haughty and did abominable things" (Ezek. 16:49–50). Sodom's main sin was failure to feed the hungry!

When teaching his disciples to pray, Jesus stressed the power of God to meet daily needs, to unshackle the oppressed, and to make peace. "To see with the eyes of the victimized is the way Christ looked at the world. It is the substance of his onesidedness, and it is exactly what led him to the cross. Take up your cross and follow me means: join the struggle. Break neutrality. Leave the wavering position in between the old and the new world."[8]

Shared Ministry

To encounter Christ in the world's sufferings is a primary concern of related modes of social ministry. But how does knowledge gained through those modes impinge on worship and prevent our "passing by on the other side"?

Suffice it to note that gathered prayer should reflect the social concerns, issue-oriented action, and mission involvements of the body of Christ in solidarity with the wounded, vulnerable, and oppressed.

The worship place is often called a sanctuary. Is it a sanctuary *from* the world or a sanctuary *for* the suffering world? Anyone whose worship service has been visited by protesters or who has heard from dissenters invited to speak from the pulpit or to share in Communion probably felt much uneasiness, if not upright anger, over the protest. Such is the seeming victory of class over cross, respectability over justice. Nevertheless the sanctuary is traditionally a place of protection from the avenging crowd.

Numbers 35 refers to cities of refuge where criminals could be protected from blood vengeance while awaiting adjudication of their cases. (The provision of sanctuary was for involuntary killers, and their cases were adjudicated by the high priest.) On the door of the Cathedral at Durham, England, is a huge door knocker that offered safety to any fleeing criminal whose hands grasped the knocker. Two priests slept above the door to admit persons who came in the night.

It is still necessary for the church to offer refuge to violators of unjust law or potential political prisoners. In that spirit, during the Vietnam war, some American congregations offered sanctuary to war resisters, deserters, etc. Unforgettable liturgy developed around the event—staying with and standing up with the pursued, breaking bread together around the table, negotiating with the authorities, becoming an advocate. The current ecumenical network of advocacy and action for human rights is in that biblical tradition, as is the underground railroad established by Christian groups to provide sanctuary for refugees from Central America.

Mission/ministry "concerns of the church," whether dramatic or ordinary, and structured opportunities to respond to these concerns are essential elements of the liturgy. Thus a congregation not only prays for political prisoners or cares for occasional individuals who are pursued, but it goes a step farther to provide space and support for organizations of political refugees. The same sequence of liturgy can develop in response to all major social concerns.

Liturgy comes alive when each member of the congregation belongs to at least one ministering group, or base community. A North American visitor to Costa Rica described how base communities worship when gathered together in larger congregations. Each base community announced what it was doing and requested counsel and assistance from others whose experience might be instructive at a different point. "The period of preparation for the prayers of the congregation became a significant high point in the morning worship. This was a time of sharing both by persons and by the base communities. Issues which had arisen from announcements were specifically included in the prayers of the congregation. In addition, those groups which may have been silent during the announcements now reported the tasks in which they were engaged. . . . Following this rather extensive period of sharing from the base groups, the entire congregation united in prayers, led by the pastor but not always exclusively voiced by the pastor. The bonds holding all the persons and groups together as the Body of Christ in this place became palpable during this time of prayer. The entire congregation stood and joined hands; everyone had bodily contact with persons, from the children to the oldest of the members. All were one in the petition of the church for the power of God to work in and through them as persons, as base communities, and as a congregation. From petitions they moved to expressions of confidence and faith in the presence and guidance of God."[9]

North American congregations also have mission groups. But how often is their work the focus of gathered prayer, of mutual support, or of congregational celebration? Worship can empower ministry directly, depending on the quality of shared concerns, succinctness of activity reports, and the mission-covenant of the congregation. Intentionality is crucial; much depends on whether or not congregational leaders believe that the church should and can bring its members out of private preoccupations into public life where cultures, classes, races, ages, sexes meet in ministry, and mutual service occurs.

If the illustrations just given seem overly task-oriented, keep in mind that liturgy is both serious and festive. Mission response can range from rallies and forums to committees and retreats, to fairs and festivals, to advocacy and service groups. Moreover, *every* gathering of the congregation *is* social. Members know and care about one another. They want to interact, to support one another, to talk and touch, to pass the Peace, not just outside the sanctuary, but in it.[10] It is not a very complicated step to extend this natural sociality to public concerns.

Leadership of worship and planning for worship are important social experiences that require careful nurture. Without violating provisions for church order, and without threatening freedom of the pulpit, it is possible systematically to share leadership in worship, and to plan together for worship. Consider the incongruity of a ministering community whose liturgists and preachers are only clergy. Most congregations are beginning to provide for some lay participation: for example, in dedicating the offering, reading Scripture, passing the Communion elements, or interpreting the mission budget. But I have in mind something more dynamic and less hierarchical.

The congregation can form planning groups, composed of members, officers, and pastor(s), to prepare for holistic worship-education-witness in each season of the Christian year. Thus there would be a group planning for Advent–Christmas, another for Epiphany and the Sundays after, another for Lent–Holy Week, another for Eastertide, and another for Pentecost and Sundays following. These groups under pastoral leadership (well in advance of the season) can study the ecumenical lectionary lessons for each Sunday in that season to identify thematic emphases for worship-education-action. Existing mission emphases interact with these concerns to make one whole approach to the congregation's Sunday life-style. The planning group for each season shares in leadership of the entire liturgy in ways that utilize its members' gifts. That way of developing a vital, participatory people's liturgy is not hypothetical; some congregations actually proceed that way. Others incorporate at least some elements of this approach.

Corporate prayer is the first social implication of God's grace. It is a primary means by which the promises of God have their way with us and with others. "Prayer," wrote Calvin, "is the principal exercise of faith"; it is the main service of the church. Prayer, and liturgy as a whole, is our first response to the radically justifying grace of God. In prayer we enjoy God's very present power to shape our lives. We receive what we ask for. In prayer, God's elected relationship with us is reconfirmed. "It is then by means of prayer that we have entered into the riches which we have in God . . .; by prayer we seek and find the treasures which are shown to our faith in the gospel."[11]

5

Liberating Bible Study and Preaching

[Theological reflection] is a catalyst for change among those who believe in the biblical promises to the oppressed, ... a process of questioning our actions and our society in the light of the eschatological message of the Bible. We begin with the *questions* that arise out of our life and out of the experience of those who cry out for deliverance; not simply with those of the "non-believer" but with those of the "non-person."
—Letty M. Russell, *The Future of Partnership*

In preaching, the spoken word interprets the written word to show the meaning of the incarnate Word. Preaching by clergy and laity makes words once spoken and written speak truthfully again with personal and public meaning.

Preaching that is biblical and spirited is *Christological* insofar as it communicates the grace of our Lord Jesus Christ, that is, "a firm and sure knowledge of the divine favor toward us, founded on the truth of a free promise in Christ."[1] It is *communal* insofar as this knowledge of God is confidently embraced and thoroughly explored by a ministering community. It is *critical* as it develops prophetic consciousness, and it is *contextual* insofar as preaching and Bible study enable us to see the relationship between the biblical situation and our own.

If the good news of salvation speaks of God at work in the world and applies to societal as well as to individual needs, what do we find in the weekly practice of preaching? Generally, not very coherent or visible social preaching; often only indirect or scattered references. Preachers rationalize their tiptoeing through public issues on the grounds that laity generally want preachers to focus on personal faith and enrichment as a means of individual and family support. Social preaching is also restrained by the notion that preaching should be personal, and therefore (false polarity) not "political." These notions still affect practitioner training to the extent that stereotyped and impoverished views of social preaching dominate the church.

A narrow view can be overcome as we explore, utilize, and appreciate three basic kinds of social preaching: interpreting current social issues prophetically, stressing Christian social values and virtues, developing a social interpretation of Scripture. All three kinds of social preaching have biblical precedent in Old Testament prophecy and in the words of Jesus. He may not have analyzed the housing crisis, but Jesus warned, "Beware of the scribes, who devour widows' houses and for a pretense make long prayers." His many parables stressed the values and virtues of the Kingdom. And he made it a point to interpret his ministry in terms of loving justice.

The three kinds of social preaching are not always distinct in sermon situations. More than one can occur in the same sermon or Bible study. The crucial thing is for preachers and hearers to become aware of the different possibilities and to appreciate how each is done.

Of the three kinds, the first is most prominent and controversial. The second is most frequent, informal, and direct. The third is most basic to the development of a whole social ministry. So I will give the third kind of social preaching the most attention in this chapter, after brief comments on the other two.

Interpreting Current Social Issues Prophetically

Proclamation that is both prophetic and pastoral, as can be seen in the Bible itself, refers to current events, examines common facts and fancies, and uses vernacular forms of speech. Disciplined theological reflection today can clarify issues and orient action in a similar way. The following ground rules for prophetic preaching or social-ethical analysis reflect the experience of expert practitioners.[2] Prophetic preaching:

—Highlights the generating power of the gospel, not moralism.

—Builds on the enormous political and social themes of the Bible.

—Requires support of a pastoral ministry that affirms the value of persons.

—Avoids direct assault on the personality and reputation of other individuals.

—Reflects homework on factual aspects and historical background of a social problem.

—Avoids unsupported references or sideswiping of controversial issues.

—Utilizes church pronouncements judiciously.

—Hits an issue straight and gives a carefully stated position.

—Summarizes the opposing point of view fairly, when appropriate.

—Uses human illustrations, but avoids stereotypes (social preaching is very personal).

—Conveys the expectation that people will change.

—Points to available ways to act constructively.

—Recognizes that Jesus, the prophets, and the disciples aroused reaction.

—Proceeds on a consensus with church officers that affirms a free pulpit over against a beholden one. creates expectation of social ministry (role validation).

structures opportunities for member feedback.
invites members to study with the preacher before,
and after, the sermon.

Stressing Christian Social Values and Virtues

The emphasis shifts from unpacking major issues to sharing basic qualities of faithfulness. What is the path of faithfulness in our time? The question that every generation of Christians asks is "answered" informally and illustratively by highlighting particular Christian values and virtues in Bible study and sermons. This is a hallmark of preaching (and liturgy, including the spirituals) in the black church. Black preaching is a method of biblical interpretation that

—Declares the gospel in the vernacular—the language and cultural idiom of the people.
—Exercises imagination which makes Bible stories meaningful to the hearers in their struggles.
—Speaks to contemporary personal-social needs.
—Draws on spiritual experience and folk wisdom.

Black biblical interpretation "puts the gospel on a tell-it-like-it-is, nitty-gritty basis. Perhaps it may happen eventually that the Word will have that much Blackness added to its connotation wherever it is used."[3]

As an example of this kind of social preaching, consider this interpretation of a favorite passage of black preachers: "You can trust God not to let you be tried beyond your strength, and with any trial to give you a way out of it and the strength to bear it" (I Cor. 10:13). The preacher, Gardner C. Taylor, emphasizes faithful virtues under personal-social pressure in this excerpt from his sermon "From Our Awful Dignity."

I preached in a certain church the other Sunday. There came down after the service a doctor who teaches in a medical school. And he came up to me, and tears came into my eyes because I remember where he came from.

He and I were born in the same town. We were born not far from a sugar plantation. . . . His father and mother, I suppose could—and I knew them—not read or write. And here he is now teaching at a medical college. He had gone to elementary schools where the terms were short. This doctor had battled his way—all of the way—I don't mean through college—I mean from elementary school on through. Seeing him brought back faces long faded and days long past.

Then he told me of how hard it had been for him. And how once he came home for the summer, not knowing whether he'd be able to go back to school or how he would get to the job out in the East that was promised to him. He did not have the money to get to the job. And he told me about a man, dearly loved of me, who let him have sixty-five dollars so that he could get back to his job, so he could go to school. He said to me, "That man did not know that right then I was at the end of my courage, and if he had not given me that sixty-five dollars, I would have given up." Now that man *did not know*—but as surely as I stand here, my faith says to me that there was somebody who *did* know, somebody who *knows* when we reach the end of our patience, some-body who *knows* when our strength has all but failed, who *knows* when we've borne the last sorrow. He is the one who cares!

Developing a Social Hermeneutic

The firm basis for all social preaching and Bible study is careful interpretation of the human-social meaning of biblical texts. Hermeneutics is the science or art of inter-preting the Bible faithfully. The word of God in the text encounters a believing community which brings current issues and contemporary dilemmas to its reading of bibli-cal words. Of particular interest here is a method of interpretation which makes clear the liberating meaning of biblical texts for human-social existence today.

Twentieth-century biblical scholarship, through form criticism, rhetorical criticism, redaction criticism, and sociological studies of biblical communities, gives us tools for a social hermeneutic. Scholars help us learn how the communities which wrote the books of the Bible handled traditional stories and sayings in relation to their life situation. Exegetes also explore the biblical author's theological purpose for modifying and connecting traditional stories or sayings as they now appear in the Bible. Some of the basic results of this historical-critical scholarship are readily available in the footnotes of the New Oxford Annotated Bible and the Revised Standard Version, and in recent commentaries.

1. The Bible itself resulted from the interaction between inherited tradition and situational viewpoint. The sociological study of biblical communities has shed more light on the situations that the biblical writers interpreted. George Mendenhall and Norman Gottwald show how Israel originated not in one conquest of Palestine, but through a series of peasants' revolts against the network of Canaanite cities and the gradual formation of a community of faith with a common oath and way of life under Yahweh.[4] The exodus narratives and the social norms of the Torah defined the character of faithfulness to this covenant in terms of an economics of equality and a politics of justice guided by a faithful free God.

Over against imperial Egypt and fatalistic Canaan, Israel developed an alternative consciousness of a God free to liberate and to be merciful to the lowliest. Premonarchical Israel was collegial rather than hierarchical, egalitarian rather than elitist. So also was the earliest church, as can be seen in the Gospels and Acts.

A "royal consciousness" emerged in Israel under kingship. It led to a religion of God's domestication, an economics of privilege, and a politics of oppression. Privileged classes dominated the social structure. Power was centralized and forced labor was levied by the royal court to build the temple. Worship a radically free God became a threat to the powerful who established a court and priesthood to control access to God, and to redefine God's demands.[5]

2. The prophets and then Jesus reasserted the earlier covenant consciousness over against the royal, priestly consciousness. They condemned the economics of privilege and the politics of oppression, proclaiming God's freedom to liberate and serve the poor. "If a prophet challenged ancient Israel, or if Jesus challenged his own Jewish, responsible contemporaries, then a prophetic reading of the Bible today should challenge those dynamically equivalent to those challenged in the text: if the priests and [false] prophets of Hosea's day or the Pharisees in Jesus' day, then the church [and economic-political] establishment today, since prophets, priests, and Pharisees represented the responsible leaders and groups of their time. Dynamic analogy also means that one reads the text for oneself and not only for others. It should not be read to identify false prophets and Pharisees with another group or someone else, but with one's own group and with oneself, in order to perceive the right text in the right context."[6]

A faithful social hermenuetic is honest to God and marked by humility and humor. "Humility means one identifies in the stories and episodes . . . with those who heard their challenging messages and learned from them. . . . Humor means that in reading the biblical texts we take God a little more seriously than usual and ourselves a little less so."[7]

3. The biblical narratives, symbols, codes, poems, parables offer words of promise, judgment, and hope that pertain to individuals (including the most pious) *and* to whole communities (including nations). In fact, communities are addressed more often than are individuals. It is important to identify and discuss the corporate, public, and political meaning of key points in a passage, as well as individual, private, and personal content.

An Example: "What Are the 'Filthy Practices'?" (Rom.

1:16–32). In the light of God's gift of grace through faith, Paul denounces all ungodliness and wickedness. But Paul's readers are likely to perceive some sins as more abominable than others. Revivalists with a personal-private perspective tend to highlight sins of personal indulgence and sexual lusts, and tend to emphasize God's abandonment of such sinners. Such an interpretation is likely to overlook Paul's intention to show that we too are sinners and have no basis for escaping judgment.

Meanwhile, a social-corporate interpretation of filthy practices would highlight the political or institutional consequences of idolatry, with particular reference to destructive philosophies and collective forms of murder, slander, propaganda, ruthlessness. Identification of social sins is consistent with prophetic consciousness which concentrates on patterns of injustice as well as personal sins. Certainly Paul was raised in that tradition, and understood that prophets such as Hosea (Hosea 1 to 3) and Ezekiel (Ezek. 16:49–50) used sexual analogies to refer to sins of oppression.

In the leadership of Bible study groups, one useful technique is to ask participants first for a personal-private interpretation of the text, and then for a social-corporate interpretation, followed by drawing some "Implications for Our Life Today." This is no more complicated an endeavor than, and at least as striking an experience as, rephrasing biblical texts in nonsexist language (a procedure that is also important in developing a liberating social hermeneutic).

One grass-roots group's personal-social interpretation of "God's Foolish Wisdom" (I Cor. 1:18–31) yielded these results:

Personal-Private Meanings

I boast in the Lord who saved me. The cross of Christ exposes my sin. I can withdraw from worldly struggle; God is on my side. God favors sinners; salvation is in the cross.

Social-Corporate Meanings

Christ upset the existing order for the sake of the lowly. Christians reject ideological justifications for corporate wealth and military policy. A power-mad and success-oriented society ignores the humanizing power of the cross. Is high technology wise? Is denuclearization foolish? Our common human weakness and social sin is the bond of humility and compassion.

A regular discipline of personal-social interpretation opens up new perspectives on familiar passages. For example, what is the primary significance of Jesus' grainfield action challenging the Sabbath? (Mark 2:23–28.) To the alienated, impoverished community of Mark, Sabbath law represented an oppressive religious-social order. By asserting the right to eat, Jesus clarified true observance of the covenant. But to the establishment, his Sabbath-breaking represented a capital offense; his disruption challenged the whole system. Not just ritualism, but ideology undergirding a class structure was involved. To which Jesus responded, the system was made for human beings, not human beings for the system.

Today, Christians face a similar struggle for bread and justice, and must decide how they will respond to oppressive policies. The church has an obligation to critique an idolized economic order in the light of biblical covenant norms. Just as Jesus justified his grainfield action by invoking the precedent of David's responsible freedom in defiance of King Saul, so the church today appeals to the Lord of the Sabbath, One greater than David, whose way has priority over the rules of existing systems.

These illustrations expose several related emphases of a social hermeneutic (i.e., principles of sociologically and ethically conscious biblical interpretation):

4. The New Testament message assumes the covenant content of the Old Testament message, as it addresses people living under political and religious oppression. People in Jesus' day had the option of going along with the

Roman imperium and the prevailing Hellenistic culture, withdrawing into secluded utopian communities, organizing a nationalistic revolt, or redefining God's covenant purpose and living out the implications. Christians chose the latter course with a sense of destiny as new people "in Christ." Their life-style featured simple liturgy, common meals, humanitarian ethics, and egalitarian structure.[8] The pressure of social forces led to disputes in the church over each of these disciplines, and tested the ecumenical covenant community. The Epistles and Gospels of the New Testament were written to interpret the new life of faith by showing its origins, and its continuity with Israel's story.

5. Liberation from oppression and poverty is a central theme of the Bible. Oppression is the subject of 300 Hebrew and Greek texts, 122 of which see oppression as the cause of poverty. "It is no exaggeration to say that 90 percent of biblical history is written from the perspective of a small, weak, oppressed poor people. . . . Latin American theologians like to point out that after the conversion of Constantine, the church (Catholic and Protestant alike) stopped reading the Bible from the perspective of the oppressed-poor, aligning itself instead with the wealthy and powerful, or at best with the middle class. That would explain why we search in vain in our multivolumes of systematic theologies and Bible encyclopaedias for articles on oppression."[9] The saving news of the Kingdom which features God's loving justice heralds a new order that epitomizes the Law and the Prophets (Luke 16:16).

6. What we bring to Scripture conditions what we draw from it. What we bring becomes more faithful when we allow the oppressed to tell us of their struggle for humanity. As we develop a view from the underside and encounter others who cry out for justice, the biblical texts speak to us with urgency, depth, and power. The texts establish an ethical basis for looking at the oppressing, exploiting systems we help to perpetuate and from which we benefit,

and for looking at oppressed, exploited conditions of others and our own lives. There is mutual hurt and dehumanization from which we, too, are liberated by opting for the oppressed. Thus, in the great reversal, the weak deliver the strong to be human again.

But we try hard to avoid the message of liberation. "We read what we can bear to read, we hear what it is tolerable to hear, and we evade (or 'spiritualize') those parts which leave us uncomfortable, if not outraged. . . . We seem to have been reading a different book from our Third World friends. For us, the Bible has generally been a book supporting and strengthening our own way of life; for them, it is a book challenging accepted values and breathing the passion of revolutionary change. . . . If indeed 'the world should not be the way it is,' how is it that we encounter Scripture (committed to the 'creation of a new heaven and a new earth') without being moved by that encounter to engage in such transforming activity? How adequate is our hermeneutics, our method of interpretation, if it leaves us complacent with the way things are, or committed only to tepid changes that fall far short of the Bible's radical demand for justice."[10]

7. The active community of faith brings to its interpretation of biblical texts an "exegetical suspicion" that important social realities have not been taken into account in prevailing interpretations of the Bible.

"If the message of justification by God's undeserved love is preached apart from an unmasking of the actual power relations which aggravated our feelings (of self-deprecation) to the level of a social neurosis; if people are released from the rat race of upward mobility only privatistically, with no critique of the economic and social ideology that stimulates such desperate cravings; if people are liberated from a bad sense of themselves without any sense of mission to change the conditions that waste human beings in such a way, then justification by faith becomes a mystification of the actual power relations, and the Christian gospel is indeed the opiate of the masses. And study of the Bible which avoids facing these issues becomes a justification of the status quo."[11]

The faithful alternative is to move among the mighty biblical texts by means of "transforming bible study" that: (a) employs the historical-critical method to defend the text from our projecting on it our own biases, theologies, and presuppositions; (b) amplifies the text by exploring its deeper meaning which is intuitively available to the faithful community; and (c) applies the text to that part of our personal and social existence which is called forth to be healed, forgiven, transformed.[12]

8. Socially critical and liberating interpretation of Scripture permits no hermeneutical suspension of the hopeful biblical ethic. Rather, a sound hermeneutic "is a process of questioning our actions and our society in the light of the eschatological message of the Bible. We begin with the *questions* that arise out of our life and out of the experience of those who cry out for deliverance; not simply with those of the 'non-believer' but with those of the 'non-person' "[13] whom the existing order ignores or overpowers.

This contrasts sharply with the traditional approach to biblical interpretation which: (a) suspends the question of contemporary theological-ethical meaning (often called "exposition") while first finding out the text's original content, structure, historical setting, theological intention, and literary form (often called "exegesis"); and (b) postpones the ethical "application" of the text until its meaning has been determined. Such an approach fosters a narrow use of historical-critical inquiry at the expense of a socially dynamic interpretation of God's Word for us today.

9. The alternative posed here is not to abandon historical-critical study, but to bring the critical tools into a larger context which also explores the human-social situation in which we read the text. We do not come to the text as

blank tablets or as people from outer space. Our occasion illumines the text and vice versa. We are already caught up in troubling human-social realities and dilemmas of faithfulness that need to be examined, that is, we need to exegete our present context. To explore this part of the context requires that we hear the voices of the oppressed, pay attention to social change advocates and read ethically informed books, periodicals, novels, and plays that offer cultural, political, and psychological analysis. To examine the human-social situation in which we read the text is as important as noting historical-critical findings of biblical scholarship.

10. At the center of all biblical interpretation is the politics of God. In each passage under study, what is the direction of God's action? How does God respond to the power or powerlessness of various people mentioned in the passage? What are the parallels today? Take the time to picture the characters in the story. Reassign the cast of characters and your place in the cast. Imagine hearing/discussing this passage in a different cultural setting or situation of powerlessness/power.[14]

Finally, biblical interpretation itself is a social act best done *communally* by mission groups and sermon preparation groups, rather than by the traditional Bible study class. Theological reflection flows out of and into public action by the community of faith. The congregation in social ministry is the locus for a liberating hermeneutic, encountering the text through action/reflection.

Using the Method

These examples pertain to a ministry of shalom.

a. Acts 19:23–27. *Confronting Idolatry in the Economic Sphere.* Who or what defines reality for you? Read the passage in our context of escalating defense spending and luxury consumption by the rich. Instead of silver shrines, think in terms of idolizing military security and superpowered weapons, as well as extravagant adornments and acquisitions. How is such economic activity justified? Compare the arguments then and now. How are you involved in idolatry of military power and consumptive living through: taxes? voting? investments? work? What did faith require of Christians in Ephesus, and what does it require of us?

b. Jeremiah 6:13–14. *True and False Peace.* (1) "Every one is greedy for unjust gain; . . . every one deals falsely." Give current examples. Imagine hearing this passage in another cultural setting. (2) "They have healed the wound of my people lightly." What kind of peace does our government seek? What kind of future did the false prophets promise as the exile approached? (3) To whom are Jeremiah's words addressed? What did Jeremiah promise to the faithful seekers of shalom? What happened to Jeremiah after he preached this Temple sermon, and how did he follow up?

c. Ephesians 2:11–22. *Christ's Reconciling Benefits.* Encounter the text, jotting down questions, for example, Why is there so much hostility between particular groups? How can the blood of Christ overcome hostility? Who is being reconciled, and what is our role in the ecumenical household? After this is done individually, enroll each participant as a member of one of the following groups (Each participant chooses which group to join):

—A group of church school teachers who want to educate children, youth, and intergenerational groups for peacemaking.
—A base community in Latin America. One of your group has just been tortured or killed by government police.
—Church members employed by a large transnational corporation or government agency whose policies are opposed by your denomination.

Each group discusses its situation and summarizes for the others. Then all three groups turn to the exegesis of the

Ephesians passage. The Bible study leader provides historical-critical background on the original problem between Jewish and Gentile Christians, and their inclusion in the household of God as a paradigm of God's reconciling work in history. "Breaking down the wall" may refer to the destruction of Jerusalem by Roman forces, since the passage was written after the fact. The "Gentiles" are literally the nations (*ethne*). Verses 13 and 14 are commentary on Isa. 57:18–19 which referred to the diaspora.

Meaning for Ministry: What barriers does Christ break and what peaceful bond of unity does Christ create? How does the mystery—hidden plan—of liberation and reconciliation become real? How does the body of Christ participate in the creation of a universal human household (*oikos*)? In a divided, violent world, what peacemaking behavior does this imply for church school teachers, base communities, transnational employees? What will it cost us to work for this commonwealth?

To summarize, this method of biblical interpretation features an honest encounter with the text, an exploration of the dual context in which the passage was written and in which we read it now, as well as an interpretation of its meaning for ministry. It is a complete action/reflection process of Bible study and exposition that begins by experiencing the text and by questioning it where we are. The process then moves to explore the human-social situation in which the Word of God encounters us. Rather than jumping to meaningful conclusions, which may ignore the Word, we pause to listen to the nuances of the text known through historical-critical scholarship. And we conclude with a fresh interpretation of what the text means concretely for the ministering community of faith today.

To participate in the dynamic reconstruction of a liberating social hermeneutic is as exciting and fundamental a task as is the development of inclusive language about God. A recognition of what a privatized, sexist church has

been missing and a recovery of a liberating social hermeneutic is of profound significance for a revitalized ministry
at the center of which is the Word of God rightly compre-
hended, preached, and heard.[15]

6

The Church
as an Educating Community

The school of Christian Living is a task concerned
with the development of the total ministry of the
congregation, not a segmented "educational" task
with one part of the church's life.
—Jack L. Seymour, "Contemporary Approaches
to Christian Education"

An early mentor in my educational ministry defined
Christian education succinctly as, "the church teaching by
what it does." Congregations are schools of Christian
living which teach by doing (or not doing) mission/min-
istry. In a milieu of vital parish life, through a process of
action and reflection, members of all ages learn how to be
faithful to God.

Christianity is caught as much as it is taught, and the
main teachers of faithfulness are persons whom we admire
or active groups in which we participate. The primary
modes of teaching are to wrestle with dilemmas of our
human-social situation under the guidance of just mentors,
and to experience a holistic congregational life-style that
dynamically links worship, nurture, and witness.

Christian education, therefore, has a purpose that is
hard to fulfill in brief weekly schooling periods, no matter
how skillfully taught. That purpose is to equip persons of
all ages to encounter the Word of God, to receive the gift of
faith, and to express basic qualities of faithfulness inside

and outside the church, that is, to learn how "to do justice, and to love mercy, and to walk humbly with God" lifelong (Micah 6:8). Whole educational ministry with this purpose nurtures a compassionate, competent community of persons who

(1) believe that there is an overall, public purpose for human life; (2) are willing to engage in the public task of seeking the specific actions required to pursue that purpose in this day and time, aware that they don't have all the answers. . . .

If Christians do believe that God has a plan and purpose for the corporate life of humankind, they have an obligation to assist the society in educating its people to fulfill that purpose. They do so directly in the education of their own people to responsible participation in the public as carriers of the vision. They educate indirectly whenever their own internal life models the vision of human destiny in God, as well as through the agency of those whose experience of that corporate life in the church sends them out into public life confident of the reality of the vision.[1]

God's faithfulness toward humanity and our responsive trust and loyalty is the subject matter of Christian education. Because faith is a covenant relation, and not a mere object of believing, the objective is to become faithful participants in a community that knows God's justice-love, cares for others, and struggles against oppression. The church's educational ministry is to nurture members in this spirit and to teach skills of response. The focus shifts from right knowledge to faithful living, or from instruction in texts of faith to action/reflection which expresses biblical consciousness.

"Once Christian education was limited to Sunday morning church schooling, with primary emphasis on Bible knowledge. Now it occurs throughout the week as education in the church community, the social community, and increasingly, in the home. Once it existed alongside the church, often as a separate building and a parallel organization. Now it is seen as an essential element of the total life of the community of the People of God, an ingredient of every ministry, gathered and scattered, a part of every kind of activity, including worship. Before it was limited to a single learning theory with primary emphasis on cognitive development. Now it includes a variety of behavioral and organismic approaches to learning with attention given to the cognitive and the affective, to beliefs and to skills, along with life-style development. Knowing and believing are no longer sufficient; living out the faith is seen as the real goal."[2]

This approach recognizes that truth is in order to goodness, communally and personally. Liberation theologies underscore this emphasis by using the word "praxis" (conscientious behavior) to refer to "the action and reflection of human beings upon their world in order to transform it."[3] Instead of domesticating participants to accept dominant values and to serve the existing order, it is a liberating, responsive pedagogy.

Action/reflection is a nonlinear process (or spiral) of awareness-analysis-action-reflection which can be entered at any point. It develops prophetic/pastoral consciousness and practical skills among the members without falling into the trap of "setting them straight" (indoctrination) or merely informing and acquiring skills (progressive education). It features education for critical consciousness and hopeful vision that enable participants to evaluate events and act courageously to change dominant systems[4]—doing the truth in love as they experience social conflict, encounter fresh claims and ideas of justice, and work for shalom.

Chapter 3 of this book specifies basic qualities of faithfulness (or shalom living) with corresponding social values that give ethical focus to Christian education. At stake is a converted consciousness and changed behavior of communities which know who and what Jesus stands for.

"Some speak of changes in 'cultural premises,' 'core values,' and 'root images.' Others call it change in 'basic assumptions and beliefs,' 'definitions of the good life,' and 'world view.' The thrust is unmistakably the same—a clarion call for more than technological fixes, more than ferreting out the structural causes of systemic disorders. *Change in the inner world of society and culture* is called for, and not only rearrangements in the vast outer apparatus, vital though that is."[5]

Implications for Christian Social Education

Education for faithfulness can no longer be viewed as an optional task of Christian education—an elective—like social ministry itself. Rather, Christian social education becomes integral to all church groups and the whole of congregational life.

For social education to become central to church education, the conventional perception of it must be discarded. In the conventional view, social education is one more elective within an elective set of educational offerings. Therefore, few adults, youth, or children get around to it. In the conventional view, Christian education remains incomplete if biblical insights are not applied to social issues, or ethical dilemmas are not exposed and discussed. But social education is not deemed to be materially necessary to the educational enterprise or to faith development. In fact, some faith development theories deliberately postpone education for justice. In the conventional view, faith is formed apart from social engagement, and social engagement is merely a consequence of faith. So belief, not social character, becomes the subject.

There is a striking parallel between a narrow perception of social preaching as having to do with prophetic stands on social issues, and a conventional view of social education as being an extra dimension of Christian education pretty much for adults only. Both conceive of faith apart from ethics—faith as a state of being rather than faithfulness as a way of life. If, on the other hand, our subject is faithfulness, then social education is central to faith development.

This is not to say that faith is only doing. It is also thinking and feeling, as ought to be evident in the action/reflection process. The community of faith is passional and rational as well as actional,[6] and all these dimensions of being are involved in lovingly doing the truth.

If the objective is social and personal conversion, through participation in a faithful community, the method is catechesis from *katechein* in Greek, literally to echo, reproduce, imitate, or pass on a lived faith. "Catechesis occurs wherever divine revelation is made known, faith is enhanced and enlivened, and persons are prepared for their vocation in the world. . . . Catechesis implies that the whole life of a congregation offers times and places in which Christian learning may occur. It is holistic."[7] The whole life of the congregation becomes the setting and occasion for Christian learning. Catechesis refers to all the ways the church forms and moves its children, youth, and adults.

The first Christians were taught by Jesus, who educated them in the true sense of the word *educare*, "to lead out." The main method of learning was for the community of disciples to follow their mentor or rabbi. Most of the important teaching happened informally, as the participants wrestled with dilemmas of faithfulness in connection with social encounter and public events, though they also utilized the Torah, the Writings, and the Prophets.

Similarly, the church teaches by what it does as the body of Christ. The most crucial learning is informal and eventful (though it may be planned). Consider how you learned that doing justice is central to Christian faithfulness. List two or three of your earliest or profoundest learning moments, specifying the Setting (Where), the Persons or Group (With Whom), and the Time in Life (When). What does your story tell about educational method and content?

In my case, I learned from the committed behavior and

thinking of leaders of groups that did something for shalom, and from the interaction between members of these groups. I was disposed to be in such groups because I had caught from Christian (missionary) parents and other teachers in the church an understanding of the inseparability of love and justice. Much of my learning has been experiential, outside of structured "school" settings, but my learning has also involved schooling moments, simulation techniques, and high-quality theological reflection in classes, retreats, and study/action groups. Learning has also occurred in times of corporate worship with groups of persons who were acting for justice and peace, in groups organizing for public action, in settings of serious study, and in communities of celebration and support.

When I consider how my children learned that doing justice is central to Christian faithfulness, I think not only of church school settings but of special events such as intergenerational participation in antinuclear or peace demonstrations, a thoroughly desegregated public school experience during a sabbatical year, work camps in a Native American setting, learning fine arts in a caring community, a summer Volunteering in Mission, a year abroad, encounters with ecumenical leaders from other countries.

"It belongs to the very essence of the gospel that we have to hear it from someone else. And it is a matter of experience that the word spoken afresh to us out of another clime or culture often comes with new power even to those who have long been accustomed to the Christian message," said Lesslie Newbigin. Keeping in mind that the word is spoken most freshly by communities that are doing the word, we realize that educational planning must make better use of learning opportunities within congregational and community life, and numerous occasions for encounter with Christians in and from other cultures (mission in reverse).

In addition to more structured cross-cultural experiences, it is essential to plan intergenerational events and involvement opportunities. In other words, we need to shift from conventional forms of compartmentalized schooling...

Toward a New Pattern of Christian Social Education

Christian educators face important choices of focus, setting, and method, here stated in terms of shifting *from* educational efforts that ... (first column) *to* educational approaches that ... (second column).

	FROM	TO	QUERIES
FOCUS	Domesticate all ages to cope rather than to change things.	Develop ethical sidedness; critical social consciousness; liberating-reconciling intentionality.	Relation between social and spiritual?
	Preoccupation with nonbelievers; love and justice; paternalism toward the poor.	Priority of the poor (nonpersons); rediscovery of biblical righteousness; a ministry of loving justice; mutuality with the powerless.	How meet personal needs? How legitimate social education?
	Stages of having faith; postpone eco-justice education.	Learn to participate in faithful community; cultivate qualities of being faithful.	E.g., life-style change resources?
SETTING	Separate educational classes by age. Nurture personal faith and fellowship.	Link worship, nurture, and action holistically, for the sake of mission/ministry.	Lectionary as unifying key? Role of pastor?
	Instruct graded groups in basic content (catechism).	Church as intentionally educating community teaching by what it does (catechesis).	How teach basic competencies?

Stay in classroom and sanctuary.	Go public, go home, and go apart in worship, nurture, action.	How get church in world and household and vice versa?

METHOD			
	Liberal, banking theory of education; study without action.	Action/Reflection cycle; attend to all parts of AAA/R.	How get from study to action?
	Age-segregated approach; denominationally isolated; routine worship.	Intergenerational and communal experience with social reality and faithful response; value-catechesis through liturgy, mission groups, use of the arts.	How do we learn? More than affective!
	Socialize individuals to adopt conventional norms.	Communal educational praxis; learning by doing, apprentices following mentors; partnership in life of justice-love.	Beware of moralism.

The whole approach charted above takes advantage of *multiple settings*, such as church, home, community, retreats, and public gatherings through a style of Christian education that links praxis with praise, preparatory study, and pastoral care. Worship, nurture, and witness are integrated in the community of persons who are grateful for God's unmerited grace, care for each other and for all, and act for justice to the poor, liberty for the captives, equity for the meek.

Ethical focus occurs as Christian education fosters prophetic consciousness. Currently, many social education efforts of local churches remain ethically unfocused because they seek to inform on "all sides" of issues, but they do not educate to act for justice. Ethical focus dissipates when all viewpoints are treated as equally valid. From a biblical point of view, special attention should be paid to the voices of the powerless and their advocates. Biblical faith gives these viewpoints preference, while recognizing that all are tainted with sin.

Therefore, it is important to "consult" *four kinds of experts* on social issues: (1) the vulnerable population and victims of a given policy, (2) the change agents who lead voluntary organizations that seek constructive changes of policy for the sake of low-power people, (3) the established powers in public office and managers of corporate entities who are responsible for administering current policy; and (4) the independent students of major public issues whose analysis is not part of a contracted service to the powers. To pay attention to all four kinds of experts without deferring to the third kind, is a hallmark of Christian social education. This guideline is as applicable to exposure experiences of children, youth, and intergenerational education as it is to adult learning.

Finally, the whole approach charted above uses a mix of *teaching/learning methods*—probing questions, pointed instruction, learning centers, a community of study and dialogue, creative arts, symbol and ritual, groups organizing for action. There is no need for silly arguments over which style is more human or less elitist. Teaching/learning is a shared responsibility involving all the methods and many available resources. Teaching involves orderly or evocative content shared amid quality experience and social change in response to real human needs. Learning involves critical questioning and hope-filled commitment to living by informed belief.

Whole educational ministry with Christian ethical focus develops as leaders of the congregation regularly link liturgical habit with Bible study and mission occasion, as can be seen in the following example. During a month of special attention to peacemaking in worship and preaching, one congregation took several educational steps on successive Sundays: (1) held an intergenerational breakfast meeting with one of our Congressional Representatives to update our public policy analysis and to express our peacemaking concerns, (2) took up the annual denominational peacemaking offering, part of which is spent in local mission, (3) conducted intergenerational Bible study of the shalom vision, (4) asked participants of all ages either to find a poem or draw a picture of peacemaking, or to write a draft letter to a member of Congress or the Administration (or the heads of government that have nuclear weapons) explaining why they oppose increased weapons buildup, and (5) concluded with an intergenerational session for sharing the letters and related pictures or poems before mailing them. Sharing began with a litany of confession for failing to make peace and concluded with a litany of intercession. The entire experience was intellectually clarifying, emotionally moving, and an active expression of group support for an urgent mission priority.

A Framework for Peacemaking Education with Adults[8]

The preceding example only begins to illumine theological-ethical content, multiple settings, and action/reflection method in Christian social education. So let me sketch the four aspects of social education method—Awareness, Analysis, Action, Reflection—with reference to the example of peacemaking. This action/reflection process is informed by the question: How do we learn to live as peacemakers amid the systemic and interpersonal violence of our time?

1. *Recover the biblical vision of shalom and retrace the outlines of the whole biblical story with awareness of this theme.* The biblical story of peacemaking encompasses vivid eschatological visions of peace and justice, the promise of shalom projected in the creation stories, images of organized violence such as the tower of Babel, the beast

and mammon, the quest for justice amid bloody conquest of Canaan, true versus false prophecies of peace, a search for real security, clashing expectations of the Messiah, Jesus' peacemaking deeds and teachings, Paul's understanding of "peace in Christ," the nonviolent life-style of the early church, and then the post-biblical movement from religious persecution to establishment, from pacifism to just war to crusade to . . .

This is a vital theological framework for worship-education-action. It needs to be explored through intergenerational experiences and communal praxis, and not just in units of study for age-graded groups. In public worship and through special events, including intergenerational retreats, congregations can celebrate the rich heritage of peacemaking and begin to learn some of the disciplines of living peacefully.

2. *Clarify the realities of the human-social situation that enhance or block shalom*, such as the revolution of rising expectations among the poor and powerless, increased defense spending by the powerful, concentrated economic control of capital and scarce resources, the communications revolution, and patterns of alienation in communities and families. Quality social analysis emerges from exposure to voices of the oppressed and courageous peacemakers, plus homework by groups of Christians who identify peaceful patterns of daily life and social policy. Such study should utilize the insights of public interest groups and investigative journalists, the research of physical and social scientists, as well as creative artists. Results of the analysis can be presented in news articles, announcements, forums, sermons, dramas, in connection with specific action opportunities.

Two realities of the human-social situation are that (1) even children can value God's love for all, make peaceful life-style choices, and develop critical consciousness about violent products, and (2) in most congregations there are church members who know the shalom vision but work in oppressive enterprises and face sharp dilemmas of Christian vocation, and who may welcome dialogue about steps to take toward good work and economic conversion.

3. *Identify specific policy choices and issue-oriented action opportunities.* This leads to public advocacy and legislative action through established ecumenical networks, to questions of responsible investment, and to opportunities for direct witness in the community. A congregation in which I participate decided through its education committee to suspend regular church school for a few weeks' emphasis on peacemaking. The "action" of each class was to prepare a display for an all-church peacemaking fair, which was open to the community. (The six-week churchwide peacemaking focus and fair also influenced ongoing church school planning.) Meanwhile, the congregation's mission committee had already decided to host a peacemaker's conference for the metropolitan area and to support ecumenical advocacy of a "nuclear freeze."

4. *Clarify middle-range norms* (in this illustration, broad foreign and domestic goals) *which comprise a framework for thinking through specific decisions.* Two basic foreign policy postures compete for public support. One emphasizes military power, national interest, and economic colonialism. The other orientation emphasizes arms control, multilateral cooperation, and economic interdependence. Both sets of goals have shaped U.S. foreign policy thinking since World War II, with sometimes one set and sometimes the other being dominant. But the second set of goals is more consistent with Christian ethics, even though it is not now the dominant orientation of U.S. policy makers. Christian education which offers a coherent social philosophy enables Christians who face policy choices and action dilemmas to evaluate their options in the light of basic Christian values and middle-range goals, and to respond accordingly.

Sound Christian education, including curriculum resources and teacher training, encompasses all four dimensions of decision-making. While particular educational plans remain situational, the four components give ethical focus to the whole approach of an educating church in a changing society.

Social Education Principles for Congregations

The following principles of Christian social education reflect the consensus of several recent seminars and planning groups which I led:

Worship

1. Incorporate social concerns into total worship experience, including liturgy, symbolic environment, music, and sermon.
2. Incorporate worship into study experiences, task forces, and action projects.
3. On holidays or days of special observance provide alternative celebrations for both home and community, stressing authentic religious values and social witness.
4. Be innovative regarding times, locations, and content of worship.
5. Introduce intergenerational participation in worship experiences.
6. For theological accuracy and clear communication, use inclusive language and symbols with regard to race, sex, age, life-style, disabilities, ethnic grouping, and other nations.
7. Nurture personal and household devotions which include meditation on the will of God for social situations and rituals of dedication to peacemaking and justice-doing.[9]

Study and Nurture

1. Improve social education in the Sunday church school, as well as in other settings, using innovative procedures.

2. Recover our biblical and theological heritage as an essential basis for social ministry, exploring it through a liberating hermeneutic (cf. Ch. 5).

3. Clearly identify basic qualities of a faithful church (cf. Ch. 3).

4. Activate small covenant or contract groups with specific (local and global) mission objectives.

5. Form intergenerational learning units, as well as graded educational groups among peers, to explore major social concerns of the church.

6. Provide resources for families and other households for strengthening communication of, and commitment to, Christian values and life-styles.

7. Provide leadership development that includes active listening, cooperative methods, responsible reflection, conflict resolution, methods of group participation, and shared decision-making.

8. Train officers and members in skills of social education and effective action in the community; give children and youth opportunities to observe socially involved adults, and to attend public events concerned with peace and justice.

9. Develop understanding of the pitfalls of paternalism contrasted with ways to empower people; provide opportunities for those being served to become our teachers in self-development, or to be missionaries in reverse.

10. Listen to leaders from other cultures and the ecumenical church; welcome plural responses from "differing but kindred minds."

11. Offer social education "extension" courses in non-church settings near or in high schools, community colleges, businesses, corporations, senior centers, camps and conferences.

Action

1. The better to involve the whole church, give a greater social action focus to whatever curriculum is

used, and celebrate social ministry in worship.

2. "Think globally and act locally," focusing the congregation's action/reflection on both local and global situations.

3. In small covenant or growth groups include action as well as study and worship.

4. Become more intentional in moving from reflection to improved social action, and also in allowing action to become a window into deeper awareness and analysis.

5. Support individuals in their beyond-the-local-church (BLC) ministry, and in on-the-job efforts to do justice.

6. Focus congregational worship-study-action on major social concerns that have denominational and ecumenical priority.

7. Work with all four components of ethical decision-making, lest specific action involvement short-circuit whole social education.

8. Give action concerns prominence in the environment of the gathered congregation—in its lore, symbols, and artistic expression.

7

Resocializing Pastoral Care and Lay Ministry

In an age which seeks private therapy for every kind of problem, we must learn that public life provides a therapy unattainable in the private realm. It is the therapy of being drawn out of one's self by interest in others; the therapy of learning that one is not alone; the therapy that comes when together we resist the conditions which say no to life and create the conditions which say yes. The church has a special opportunity to help at this point, for so many come to the church seeking private counsel for their ills. But the church stands in a tradition which affirms that to seek your life is to lose it, while to lose your life in service to God and in others is to find it. The public life gives us the chance to lose ourselves in others and thereby find ourselves healed and whole again.

—Parker J. Palmer, *Going Public*

PASTORAL CARE AND COUNSELING

Three questionable assumptions underlie much recent writing about pastoral care: that pastoral care is directed *to* members of the congregation, that it is done *by* professional clergy, and that the best model for pastoral care is clinical psychology applied mostly *through* counseling and chaplaincy. When one refers to "pastoral ministry" today, the prevailing image is of pastors shepherding persons who are already in the fold, by means of clinical counseling.

Several practical theologians have criticized the clinical pastoral education movement for its indifference to theological norms, its anti-intellectual stress on feelings and emotions, its upper-middle-class bias, its lack of attention to the social dimensions of personal troubles, and its fondness for one-on-one counseling at the expense of both Christian education and social action.[1] While the movement has helped to humanize pastors and other church leaders by enabling them to help others become more psychologically self-aware, it has deflected attention from a whole ministry of shepherding.

"The pastoral care movement has been eminently successful in recruiting pastors out of the church, and out of pastoral care, into clinical care. It has been less successful but still influential in diverting pastors from the acquisition and practice of pastoral skills to clinical skills while remaining within the pastoral context. The movement has failed to facilitate and enlarge the roles and functions of pastoral care. . . . We have tended to look upon the church and the clergy as the handmaidens of the mental health movement per se, and thereby fail to look at the particular and special contributions of the church and clergy in the overall context of the society."[2] This critic suggests that the pastoral care role can be revitalized by concentrating on the church itself as a social system that responds to ongoing human needs, and by caring for people through interventions that help to change the pressures upon them.

The church as a social system can become an effective community of moral discourse, a learning-growth center that leads forth into newness, a nurturing-preserving fellowship, or reparation center, and a source of empowerment which prevents demoralization and nurtures responsible freedom. The congregation active in society becomes the locus for and doer of pastoral care. The primary role of professional church workers is to equip a faithful *community* to intervene compassionately in the social system and to enhance caring interpersonal relations in ways that are consistent with Christian maturity. The subject matter for leadership development in pastoral care shifts from a preoccupation with interpsychic plumbing to a study of moral theology, social psychology, and power analysis. To develop the congregation's capability to do more effective pastoral care requires a working knowledge of personal, family, group, and community dynamics (each of which has a life cycle). One must explore the cultural, economic, and political determinants of human behavior, as well as skills of human interaction, crisis intervention, and social action.

This approach recognizes that people are messed up because they lack clout as much as confidence. "There are people who have been brutalized by inhuman housing, by police harassment, by the failure of the medical delivery system. There are people who have been *marginalized* because they are not needed at the moment by the economic system. There are people who have been *anesthetized*, whose jobs and lives are fundamentally alienating."[3] In other words, pastoral care must pay attention to the social field of forces including pathological ideologies and institutional environments which shape our existence, and not simply our internal organization as persons. For example, pastoral counselors have only recently grasped the fact that women are *socially* disadvantaged and that their alienation cannot be treated on the basis of individualistic psychology, but only by participation in action to deal with sexist oppression and economic victimization. Real therapy is not to be confused with passive adjustment to the status quo.

A social approach to pastoral care proceeds as congregations learn how to affect power and systems as much as (and for the sake of) personal spiritual well-being. That precisely is the difference between individual counseling and family systems therapy. The latter focuses on distress or health in the household and its impact on all the members. The same logic and method is applicable to church and community organizations.

Key Biblical Leads

The Gospel of John fosters an egalitarian, dynamic, in-but-not-of-the-world concept of shepherding or pastoral care, in the context of Jesus' claim to be the Way.

> I am the door; if any one enters by me, he [or she] will be saved, and will go in and out and find pasture. The thief comes only to steal and kill and destroy; I came that they may have life, and have it abundantly. I am the good shepherd. The good shepherd lays down his life for the sheep. He who is a hireling and not a shepherd, whose own the sheep are not, sees the wolf coming and leaves the sheep and flees; and the wolf snatches them and scatters them. He flees because he is a hireling and cares nothing for the sheep. I am the good shepherd; I know my own and my own know me. . . . I have other sheep, that are not of this fold; I must bring them also, and they will heed my voice. So there shall be one flock, one shepherd. (John 10:9–16)

The Shepherd, we are reminded, has a universal intent, consistent with the purpose of the preexisting Word. Authentic pastoral care in the light of this Word protects the sheep against "the wolf" (oppressors?), and cares very much for sheep beyond this fold. "One flock" under one shepherd is *all the people of the known world.* This cosmopolitan world coming together is signified through the ecumenical unity of believers who are working for the common good.

Jesus' discourse in the Gospel of John, following Ezekiel, portrays a comprehensive, conflict-laden ministry of the Shepherd, who cares especially for the weak, sick, crippled, strayed, and lost, and keeps them from becoming food for all the wild beasts (Ezek. 34:1–16). The ethical intention is "to feed them in justice . . . and to make with them a covenant of peace" (34:16b, 25a).

Shepherding in the tradition of Ezekiel and John links pastoral care with prophetic politics.[4] The authentic shepherd is a steward of God's justice and peace for the sake of abundant life in all kinds of social relations and in all times of the life cycle.

First Peter 5:2–3, written in a setting of intensified persecution and ecclesiastical hierarchy, also charges presbyters or church leaders to tend the flock of God in exemplary fashion consistent with the work of the Chief Shepherd. While the flock here refers mostly to church members, the passage conveys a sense of the whole dimensions of pastoral care.

What kinds of pastoral care ought congregations to undertake? Today's congregations often assist pastor(s) through direct visitation or helping services to members and a few others in need. Recently there has been a movement to train lay visitors to do preliminary personal counseling and to offer structured friendship especially to older members who have limited mobility, or are shut in, as did the commissioned widows in I Tim. 5:9. This helps to reduce the case load of the clergy, but it may not venture very far into the social dimensions of pastoral care.

Even among the deacons, or parish social service group, there has been much less attention to intervention or advocacy in the systems of health care, housing, criminal justice, and employment than there has been personal visitation with those who are facing serious problems on these fronts. Such pastoral care is a source of immediate help and significant information. But by itself it may perpetuate dependence instead of fostering liberation. As one parish visitor commented: "It's almost like we need dependent people to feel significant ourselves. Don't we want something more from each other and the church? Can we learn better ways to receive and give mutual help in the direction of faithfulness?"

People are nourished and sustained through quality engagement in ministry with and for others. Social involvement can be a rewarding and enriching experience which helps persons mature. A choice between personal growth and social change is unnecessary; they develop together through an adequate ministry of pastoral care.

A Covenant Group for Communal Pastoral Care

Perhaps the most effective pastoral care is offered by congregations that structure themselves into apostle groups, mission groups, or fellowships for service to others as well as for mutual care.

Even short-term groups that form to deal with a major concern, such as life-style change, can do mutual pastoral care, provided that the members develop a degree of trust. A useful model is offered by *A Covenant Group for Lifestyle Assessment*,[5] the title of an ecumenical adult curriculum resource that has received considerable use in Presbyterian, Methodist, Episcopalian, American Baptist, and United Church of Christ congregations. Users of this participant's manual form a support group of persons who come together over a period of months, on the basis of promises to each other and with the intention to help each other see, accept, and enjoy appropriate life-style changes. The group explores a new, flexible standard of sufficiency, which links distributive justice with abundant community, and takes up opportunities for life-style change in consuming, conserving, eating, sharing, giving, playing, working, advocating.

Each session of the group begins with sharing "good news" of actual changes made or insights gained (a familiar technique in group counseling), and it moves toward self-aware life-style analysis, utilizing discussion, Bible study, liturgy, journal-keeping, and opportunities for public policy action. It is a whole approach to pastoral care that is both personal and political in focus, occurring in a community of persons that covenants to care for one another in wrestling with personal dilemmas and exercising responsibility. Anyone who has been through this process knows how much it can expose what we really value and ways to change in the direction of sufficiency, stewardship, and solidarity.

The illustration: (1) shows that pastoral and prophetic activity are not contradictory roles, as conventionally assumed; (2) combines interpersonal and social policy dimensions of pastoral care; (3) assumes that groups of people can learn how to come to grips with cultural changes and political forces that impinge directly on their lives; and (4) underscores the strength of the church when several modes of ministry are combined holistically in a community of support. In one scheduled activity we see the importance of a liberating hermeneutic, of action/reflection learning, and of a support group that accepts participants and encourages them to be accountable to one another in common obedience to the gospel. The example is in the tradition of early Calvinism, of Anabaptist Brethren, of Methodist class meetings, of new mission churches overseas, and of recent movements for civil rights, peace, and women's equality.

"To build a moral community [without being moralistic] is to contribute to health. To help establish the value framework for right action is to contribute indirectly to health. To minimize value confusion, to clarify the objects and values worthy of people's loyalty, is to contribute to their emotional and mental well-being. Hence, it is of utmost importance for the minister and the entire congregation to develop . . . a sense of [ethical] tradition. . . . An organic sense of *style*—of the way 'we people are'—is fundamental if a community of moral discourse is to become a community of action. Such a style is important if pastoral care is to transcend remedial counseling and become a matter of incorporating people into a moral world that actually commands attention and influences thought and action."[6]

Pastoral Care of Structures

The tradition of the cure of souls also assumes the need for pastoral care of the community organically, or structurally. The literature on urban ministry in the 1960s recovered some fuller meanings of this concept, with special reference to the public role of the clergy. More than a decade later, I perceive three basic dimensions to pastoral care of structures: caring for community structures, attending to care structures, and leading (or caring for) anxious congregations.

Caring for Community Structures

In this ministry, clergy and laity concentrate on preventive and constructive activity to strengthen community morale and to quicken community life. This means being present with, and helping to lead, a diverse range of civic organizations, business and professional groups, educators, parents, and social action organizations, community service agencies, adult and youth activities centers, political clubs, etc.

One pastor of a lower-middle-class congregation "between the fats and the flats" in Oakland, California, described this style of ministry as follows:

Our objective is to foster spiritual growth through worship, education, fellowship, community involvement, continuing programs for all ages, assistance in hard times, including counseling and food and clothing when needed. In the larger community we seek to improve the quality of education, housing, business, recreation, police protection, and community morale as a whole.

Effective ministry depends on power analysis, acceptance of conflict, and organizational participation by clergy and laity. The church should be both a community center and a vigorous presence in community associations. The style of ministry is to be a visible, accessible community resource both personally and institutionally. We are a resource to structures as well as to people in a defined parish. That way we know who needs what kind of help and where they can really get it.

I came to this with experience in political science, community organization, and commercial activity. We buy ad space in the community newspaper for our overall program and for our referral services. In the Yellow Pages we also list our program groups and forms of assistance such as welcoming organization, personal service bureau, resource for ex-offenders, and age-specific listings. We staff a 24-hour answering service as well as emergency services.

Community groups meet here rent-free. We also foster special programs, plays, music, and art happenings. Our major advocacy effort now is to influence the administration and curriculum of the public schools through a group of school professionals and parents we organized and which meets here. My time is distributed as follows, by action of the Session:

10% Worship of God (I study the lectionary with a group of pastors)

30% Inreach, including nurturing and pastoral visitation of members

10% Outreach, including service to the larger church

40% Service to Community, as described above

5% Youth Activities (action/reflection for responsible adulthood)

5% Leadership Development

Administration is spread across these categories, and we present our annual budget to show how it is spent for these program categories.

Attending to Care Structures

This is a more specialized step, oriented to strengthening the community resources for mutual help in families, churches, neighborhoods, and social groups, and to challenging the policies and patterns of heavily bureaucratized, professionalized, and institutionalized "care" services.

Ministry with professionals and administrators in the caring profession, as well as with community groups that want to establish better services can: (1) unmask the ideology of service systems that confuse genuine service with care, and that create clients and monopolize markets; (2) direct critical attention to structures of power and control over service delivery systems; (3) organize the powerless to help define, and manage relevant services (e.g., preventive community health systems); (4) clarify what are necessary human services in a situation of declining public resources; and (5) support a variety of efforts to develop alternative understandings and expressions of "care and help."[7] Some of this activity moves into the arena of community organization and development, but we begin with a pastoral care problem: to whom do we refer people in need, given the lack of help available and the patterns of disservice that are so prevalent in the "caring" professions and "human service" bureaucracy? Attending to the care structures is a way to respond to the crisis that no amount of one-on-one counseling or personal crisis care will meet. Training for this dimension of pastoral care is still hard to come by; there is wisdom to share among ministering clergy and laity who have learned by doing.

Leading Anxious Congregations

Often in most urgent need of pastoral care are congregations as systems which face major dilemmas of mission priority or find their surrounding community going through rapid transition. Congregations or their subgroups are likely to behave pathologically when institutional survival itself is threatened, as is happening to a growing number of congregations under the pressure of stagflation and demographic shifts. The denial and bitterness expressed in this circumstance can be overwhelming. Congregations must move through the stages of *denial* and *anger* about the institutional crisis, and beyond *guilt, bargaining,* and *depression,* to an acceptance of the death of prevalent ideological myths and institutional forms, and a birth of more appropriate forms. But "something must give" in the current institutional pattern, if there is to be a rebirth of ministry.

One can hardly imagine struggling congregations staying healthy through the lean years, unless major institutional changes occur to reduce one or more of the following: building overhead, staff costs, program of ministry, or mission giving and action. Generally, the order of reduction or simplification has been just the reverse of the order in which the previous sentence lists the options: first, cut mission giving, then reduce program of ministry, then move to part-time staff, and finally close the building. For many members, the church *is* the sacrosanct building where they worship, or have fellowship, or experience rites of passage. Nevertheless, the *present* building, or at least the way it is presently being used, is often the *least* essential aspect of being a congregation in mission. Far more important is the mission purpose, the pattern of ministry, and competent leadership. Congregations do need identifiable places to gather, but do they need monuments more than tents?[8]

When one recalls that congregational life began with the dispersed synagogues that were formed during the exile after the Babylonian destruction of the Temple in Jerusalem, it is all the more appropriate to think in terms of less costly, semipermanent sanctuaries or multipurpose buildings for worship, nurture, and witness. God's Spirit and mission in the world is not dependent on any auspicious gathering place, as Ezekiel emphasized in his vision of the winged chariot (Ezek. 10 and 11). The options for reducing overhead are not limited to maintaining or closing the facilities we have. Other possibilities include two or more congregations sharing one place, renting space, or moving much of the church's life into a house church pattern, reserving some buildings for "cathedral" occasions.

We can also expect considerable movement toward "tentmaking" ministry or dual-role clergy, with congregations paying less than full-time staff and requiring more lay leadership. Few clergy or congregations, however, are prepared for this future. There will be an almost overwhelming temptation to turn dual-role clergy into part-time chaplains of congregations with shrinking membership, attendance, resources, and program, *unless* leaders of congregations become much more articulate about, skilled in, and mutually supportive of shared mission/ministry. A clear choice of strategy emerges: *either* attempt to preserve a shriveling pattern of church life that tries to maintain congregations with high overhead and staff costs, *or* redevelop congregations more organically in terms of the social modes of ministry sketched in this book.

EMPOWERING LAY MINISTRY

If there is only one call of God in Jesus Christ extended to all persons, those who respond to the call all become ministers or servants whether they are functioning as laity or as clergy.... The ministry is part of that one call as each and every Christian is set free for others, set free to serve now in and through many communities and situations. (Letty M. Russell, *The Future of Partnership*)

Twentieth-century theology has rediscovered that social vocation and mutual ministry are basic to the existence of all Christians, rather than options only for some Christians. The golden text for a revitalized doctrine of mutual ministry, of course, is Eph. 4:1–16, which affirms one baptism and call expressed through a variety of gifts to be apostles, prophets, evangelists, pastors, and teachers "to equip the saints for the work of ministry, for [edifying] the body of Christ" toward the goal of "mature [humanity]."

This vision has been institutionalized to some degree in the Society of Friends, the Sunday School Movement, volunteer mission societies, and women's organizations. In fact, much social ministry is actually done by talented lay women (though the need to work has drastically reduced volunteer time). No doubt, women were routed in this direction, or chose this outlet for activity beyond the home, in a world and church run by men. Some men also enter into challenging underpaid forms of social ministry (e.g., community organization and development, poverty and hunger action, child and family justice, peacemaking ministry) and do question the standard career path for professionals. Moreover, couples in ministry are creating new forms of service to church and society. Crucial to this movement toward partnership is a relinquishment of hierarchical power and learning to give in ministry, rather than struggling one more time to gain status.[9]

Yet on the subject of empowering lay ministry, much more is said than done. "Old habits of dominance and dependence persist. While the idea of full colleagueship in ministry may sound attractive in the abstract, it soon becomes disturbing and even threatening, to lay persons as well as clergy, when concrete steps are taken to make it a reality in practice."[10]

The confusion and threat focus on several components: (1) a changed relationship between clergy and laity which reduces the dominant status of clergy and increases the responsibility of the laity; (2) a recovery of the vocation of the laity to change the structures and practices that feed injustice; and (3) the need for clarity about the multiple settings or channels for ministry.

Seminars on lay ministry still indulge in quite a bit of rhetoric about clergy dominance and irrelevance. Laity who have grasped the vision of mutual ministry feel blocked by "clergy who want to control the direction of the church and who refuse to share power." This is a legitimate complaint, though it is made by persons who have socially regressive as well as progressive goals in mind. Certainly the clergy club needs to change its behavior and open doors in the direction of shared leadership and decision-making power. But in my view, this is not the main barrier to empowering the laity for ministry in the world. Far more significant is clergy and lay uneasiness about a shared *social* vocation, and the tendency of internal congregational life to co-opt the time of both.

For the most part, Christians (including clergy) are unwilling to risk their advancement or even loss of employment in order to challenge the commitments of the institutions where they are employed. That is not a clergy versus laity problem. It is a mutual vocational crisis. "Throughout Scripture, vocation means the call to service in meeting vital human needs. . . . Consistently this call has meant abandonment of the comfort and security of the *status quo* in order to respond especially to urgent human needs that existing institutions have neglected."[11] Jesus decisively rejected distortions of his vocation, and in teaching and healing he strove to humanize insensitive and unjust institutional structures. Similar responsibility and risk are at the base of contemporary ministry.

The people of God share a ministry in three dimensions: "(1) a ministry *by lay people* in their political, occupational, social and other in-the-world institutional relationships, enabled by the clergy; (2) a ministry *through* the institutional church in its service, mission and social action programs, supported by the contributions (financial and personal) of lay people; and (3) a ministry *within* the institutional church, carried on mainly by trained professionals (the clergy), assisted by volunteer lay people."[12] I will concentrate on the first of these dimensions, since the second dimension (*through* the church) is treated in the modes of ministry delineated in Chapters 8 and 9, and the third dimension (*within* the church) was treated in modes of ministry discussed above, from liturgy through pastoral care.

The ministry of lay people in secular institutions is given least attention in the gathered life of the congregation. Yet it is the most important dimension of lay ministry by the people who are called "not to be served but to serve" . . . "outside the fold," where they spend most of their time, as workers, community participants, citizens, and consumers.

Recent lay ministry training has focused upon the need for a *support group* of several persons who are acquainted and who affirm: "Yes—I see my Christian vocation as working to change the organizations in which I labor or participate. Yes—I want the support of others who have a similar sense of vocation rooted in values of the Christian faith."[13]

In my experience, these support groups of from eight to twelve persons "validate" gifts of ministry, identify strategies of organization change, and begin to develop some mutual accountability. Participants receive emotional/moral fellowship (or koinonia) through worship, study, and sharing. They also move in the direction of creative problem-solving and help participants do a strategic analysis of where the power lies and who their allies are in changing an organization. They can also experience personal "highs" of rejoicing and commiserating.

But there is a problem with this approach. It very easily shifts into the familiar ruts of personal growth groups or training for organizational leadership. Many lay ministry support groups become self-centered and fuzzy about their social vocation. When the group fails to grapple with the main goal of lay ministry, and centers instead on the sharing of personal feelings and organizational development techniques, there is a marked tendency toward self-condemnation or self-justification, or both together.

If our efforts to call forth the gifts and to share the power of ministry are to have healthier outcomes, several steps need to be taken:

1. Let us reduce the rhetoric and explore basic on-the-job ethics in our efforts to empower lay ministry. This is especially important in occupationally mixed groups which do not exist to do mission together, but only to support each other in their individual ministries. Members of short-term mixed groups can matriculate into more action-oriented groups which are not as likely to be self-centered. The core curriculum for mixed groups includes

study of the Bible (the *church's* book), current books on a theology of lay ministry,[14] and portions of this book on social ministry.

The core curriculum should also venture into the ethics of economic life, since a basic skill of lay ministry is to be informed by Christian faith in decision-making on the job and in community politics. Without claiming that there is a Christian economics which is being practiced by this or any other society of sinners, it is possible and helpful to identify core biblical values that shape a Christian perspective within which to judge and shape economic life. Four guidelines from Christian faith for economic life are:

A notion of *material sufficiency* or "enough" (in contrast to unlimited production and maximum consumption).

An understanding of *stewardship and dominion* as gentle caring extended to all creation (in contrast to a "species chauvinism" on the part of humans, and a sense of time that takes in only the current generation).

An understanding of *universality and equality* as important base lines for an economic order (in contrast to exclusion of particular human groups from either benefits or burdens of economic life).

An understanding that *human sinfulness* calls for checks against large aggregations of economic [and political] power (because of the human propensity to use power in narrowly self-interested ways).[15]

Basic to the empowerment of lay ministry is the development of critical consciousness about the ideology and behavioral tendencies of the economic system. The objective is to learn to ask the right questions and to make ethical decisions in the light of Christian faith.

2. Well-designed support groups to empower lay ministry are likely to crystallize the vocational crisis of some participants (to the consternation of others). Many people are now seeking better work opportunities as well as a restructured workplace. Underemployed persons, espe-

cially, want to find good work that genuinely serves others and is conducted in a satisfying way. Good work in this dual sense is hard to find; in an overdeveloped society it is becoming quite scarce.

Creating or reshaping one's own job is an uncertain enterprise, an invitation to rejection, disappointment, even poverty. Support from the church in the form of personal support, help in developing skills, assistance in opening doors, etc., is crucial. It is also a rather novel area of congregational involvement, since congregations have been more in the habit of caring for members before and after work than in helping them find and do good work. People can develop social ministry as a life's work, or a few years' work, that is fulfilling but not lucrative. Young and old alike who are being left out of the current work system, or are repelled by some of its methods and products, await congregational leadership in the direction of good work. "People who create their own jobs find their work stimulating and exciting. Even the prevailing view of vocation in our society expresses recognition of the need for interesting work. . . . But the Gospel recognizes a deeper truth in human nature. We find fulfillment in using our creative powers to meet human needs."[16]

3. Most adults in the church will be disinterested in the previous option, either because they are reasonably happy with the work they have, or dare not leave their "secure base" of current employment. How can these members of the church be "deployed" in ministry? The answer is that they are already deployed, but need to coalesce in mission with support and assistance from the congregation and ecumenical groups.

The pattern of lay ministry which these persons can most effectively pursue is the sector-oriented task force or mission group. Such a task force focuses on a particular sector of work such as health care, public education, social welfare, housing policy, problems of plant closings, responsible industrial development, and the media. Each task force should be made up of persons who have concern for this sector of work and its social effects. But the membership of the group should *not* be limited to those who work in that sector. The task force should also include persons with volunteer time to do homework, to participate in dialogue, and to develop the outsider's strategy of action while the workers implement an insider's change strategy.

This sector-focused approach recognizes that institutions and professions are called to ministry and have unique gifts to contribute to the common good. Organizations and people need to develop structures of action for justice and networks of personal support and accountability. Therefore, sector-oriented groups may want to meet at or near appropriate workplaces.

4. At the same time such groups must not be naive about the possible consequences. When we cross the threshold of the workplace, we seem to lose our human rights, or the organization tries to preempt them. Out of a sense of conscience and Christian commitment, one corporate executive, for example, became involved in changing the work environment. He made significant internal changes in his unit by hiring people with common commitments and values and by changing his leadership style. But he and the entire unit were fired en masse because they contradicted the "order" and policy of the corporation, so he made a career change in order to gain personal control of responses and behavior in the workplace. He chose real estate. The work was not as satisfying. He and his family moved to a different community to get a fresh start. Now he still earns money in the business sector, but he concentrates his energy for ministry in the voluntary sector. He heads a task group in the congregation which offers lukewarm support. (Labor leaders, similarly, have found little congregational support.)

The story could be repeated many times. It is hard to make significant changes in the places where we work and the products we make or sell. The same barriers to change exist in professional arenas. Therefore we need to be in lay ministry groups that include people from our work sector and people who are concerned but not directly involved. Above all we should avoid forming lay ministry groups within the same organizational hierarchy!

One example of constructive lay ministry development which I helped to launch was a series of consultations which included professors and ministers in land-grant universities (and nearby hunger action leaders) concerned with agricultural research and extension policies worldwide.[17] The national and regional meetings also included participants *not* employed in agricultural schools but aware of their ethos.

We began by clarifying our common *purpose* in the light of the biblical justice imperative. We explored some dimensions of agriculture's systemic *problem* of economic concentration, driving people off the land, coupled with skewed research and training priorities, and development of sometimes inappropriate technology. We looked at the many ways in which the difficulties of the poor countries and regions relate to the behavior of relatively rich institutions with displaced goals, ecological myopia, disdain for grubby labor, and disregard for the fragile, the small. Not only is "their" problem "our" problem; what the poor need in a dramatic way becomes our need. For our agriculture is caught up in a cost-price squeeze, spiraling capital debts, an ecological bind, and desperation to produce ever more "efficiently" in order to keep up. The present pattern has become a no-win game for most people. Changes in the direction of eco-justice would mean benefits for all but the few who now reap short-term profits.

A reconstruction of the agricultural mission of both university and church requires the best *professional* expertise with a clear analysis of the problem and ethically focused purpose. This raises some sharp dilemmas. As one professor of agricultural economics said in a follow-up regional gathering, "I have to choose between satisfying the academic profession and dealing with the social problem, and I am choosing to work on the agricultural development problem and its political-economic causes." His statement of vocational consciousness was met with admiration and uneasiness.

This vignette merely indicates what can and ought to happen among groups of Christians who are exploring their vocational responsibility and policies of justice in major sectors of work. It may be argued that the average congregation does not have the competence to follow through with the kind of task groups I recommend. Yet, several resources are available to congregations. Among the participants are lay persons who are experts concerning their work setting. Other participants in these task forces have expertise in community leadership and organizing, as well as knowledge of community needs. The congregational or ecumenical group with its built-in resource of expert church members also has the asset of specialized community ministers, campus pastors, or institutional chaplains who have learned how to relate Christian faith to particular institutions or sectors of work. And there is one more important resource: the local group's direct access to community decision-making and resources. A local task force with a clear justice agenda has more lay ministry power than does a support group that gathers within one company or a geographically diffuse consultation such as I described in the example.

5. Finally, congregations have a liturgical responsibility to pray for workers in various occupations—all kinds of workers, not just the elite. Prayers for God's empowerment of the people give focus to lay ministry. Mark Gibbs recalls receiving "almost embarrassing thanks" for offering just such a pastoral prayer while leading a worship service in a village church. "I prayed explicitly for the local police, the storekeeper, and innkeeper. In my inno-

cence I had assumed that such would be normal practice. It had in fact never occurred within living memory."[18]

Some congregations also plan occasional rites of vocational rededication. While this liturgical concept is useful, available printed liturgies leave much to be desired in their lack of justice focus or safeguards against exclusive use. In liturgy that highlights lay ministry, beware of reinforcing status consciousness and of discriminating against the unemployed or underemployed including those who chose or are forced to stay home. Avoid rituals that recognize particular elite groups such as doctors, business leaders, educational administrators; keep a broad vocational focus in the liturgical recognition of vocation. "Just as Jesus called his disciples away from their conventional occupations [whatever their social status], so we are called not to choose among existing jobs, but to choose among existing needs."[19] An appropriate liturgy will undergird the people's power and responsibility to minister in daily work, political and economic activity, and community life—concerns and opportunities that include everyone.

8

Renewal of Community Ministry

Show no partiality [to the rich and do not dishonor the poor] as you hold the faith of our Lord Jesus Christ, the Lord of glory.

—James 2:1

We ask for the church's presence with us, beside us, Christ among us. We ask for the church to sacrifice with the people for social change, for justice, and for love of neighbor. We don't ask for words; we ask for deeds. We don't ask for paternalism; we ask for servanthood.

—César Chavez

SOCIAL SERVICE—ADVOCACY

Provision of direct services to meet human need is a prominent mode of congregational ministry that receives warm support because it shows direct results without necessarily raising systemic issues (though it should). Congregations typically spend part of their local mission money or take special offerings to support services that provide food, shelter, relief, education, recreation, counseling, health care, visitation, rehabilitation, resettlement, crisis intervention, etc. Some congregations effectively utilize public and private resources to undergird their social service. Denominations and ecumenical agencies also raise millions of dollars to fund service projects and to field mission personnel with particular medical, educational, agricultural, social development competencies.

Who can doubt the need for such services and the obligation of Christians to offer them without paternalism or proselytizing? The question is not whether the church should do more social service, but what kind, with whom, and by what means? Careful exploration of the question is all the more important now that public resources to meet basic needs and to support civic amenities have been cut back—severely eroding governmental and nonprofit service programs and lowering the quality of life for all.

A reduction in public resources for social service also hampers private programs, since many community services involve nonprofit groups in a contracted relationship with public agencies and the United Way. While congregations and regional church bodies can do more than they are doing to meet community needs and to house community organizations, it is naive to imagine that churches along with other voluntary groups can take up the slack or fill the huge gap created in human services by the tax revolt and inordinate military spending. A few more alternative schools for a couple hundred students hardly resolves any city's crisis of public education. Another food pantry does not meet the underlying need for adequate income or good nutrition. As more victimized, powerless people seek help from the staff of congregations and church-supported community agencies, what is the church's responsibility?

Authentic, Competent Christian Service

The parable of the Last Judgment (Matt. 25:31ff.) evaluates the faithfulness of nations and groups by their service of "the least." Empowering Christian service is also prominent in Jesus' answer to John's disciples who ask for proof of his messiahship. "Go and tell John what you have seen and heard: the blind receive their sight, the lame walk, lepers are cleansed, and the deaf hear, the dead are raised up, the poor have good news preached to them" (Luke 7:22). The teachings and healings of Jesus are signs of the new humanity which God creates to displace the old order. *Especially* in his response to the poor and the sick, Jesus reveals the power of God. His followers also adopt a life-style of simplicity, sharing, and healing service, which startles the public and threatens the authorities (cf. Acts 3 and 4).

Two things are quite apparent in the biblical view of service. First, authentic service (diakonia) has the objective of liberating persons and groups from miserable conditions. Second, service is valuable in itself, not simply as a means to increasing adherents. Christians therefore should be concerned to develop quality social services that empower people, without regard to how many persons are brought into church membership. Authentic Christian service is not to be confused with "Christian missions" which demand body counts of "souls saved" or which refuse to clearly distinguish between funds spent for social services and funds spent for proselytizing or administration.

1. The first sign of Christian service is a bridging of class cleavages and racial-ethnic diversity in common action to meet human need—in other words, wherever Pentecost happens and people act for the common good. For middle-class churches to move in this direction is a major life-style change.

A further implication of inclusive service is to bridge the barriers of religious difference through interfaith action to meet human need. The churches of Washington, D.C., for example, incorporated an Interfaith Conference of Protestant, Catholic, Jewish, and Islamic faith communities which has task forces on aging, employment, housing, and hunger. Many congregational leaders in this interfaith conference for the first time fully encountered and worked with people of other faiths. Each congregation provides leadership, money, and volunteers for this community conference which coordinates the human service efforts of many congregations.

Signs and symbols of healing the sick, the lame, lepers, and casting out demons are as important as the Word proclaimed through preaching (Luke 9:2). How can the church's own life become a sign of healing rather than a sign of decay? Where should limited resources and energy be focused to show the healing power of the gospel in the local community?

2. A healing ministry is as interested in the causes of social problems as it is in the effects. It deals with pervasive conditions (e.g., the shortage of decent affordable housing) as well as immediate challenges (individuals who need housing). A healing ministry in society works directly with persons facing hunger, illness, unemployment, lack of shelter, family crisis, public assistance, hassles, etc. It also seeks to reduce the recurrence of these crises by organizing to advocate better public policies and to improve community services. Thus, in response to particular conditions, such as inadequate housing, churches work on a case-by-case basis with persons who need housing. Churches can also study the patterns and causes of housing problems, monitor the administration of existing policies, organize alternative mechanisms such as cooperative or shared housing, and advocate policy changes that would relieve the housing crunch. A healing ministry encompasses both kinds of response.

3. Service involves stewardship of resources: buildings, people, talent, organizational energy, commitment to the poor, hope for a viable future. These resources need to be gathered, focused, and shared for the common good. One important community service during leaner years is to offer church buildings for use by community groups at minimum expense.

Service is enhanced by holding more things in common (Acts 2:44) and distributing them according to need (Acts 4:35). Especially as suffering increases globally and locally, the church's habits of service must change to overcome duplication and laissez-faire do-goodism, while enhancing more cooperative, competent ministry for the larger community good.

Some practical models of church-based social service are the following:

—Buildings in large and small cities are natural locations for community centers, with a variety of community groups using the facilities for cooperative gardening, recreation, child development, adult education.

—Older members of congregations often own homes that are too large for them to live in alone. Churches can provide the education and technical services to create shared, intergenerational housing as an alternative to age-segregated retirement homes.

—Many congregations participate in sponsoring refugee families, in programs of prison visitation, in group homes and activities for retarded persons or delinquent youth, etc. These congregations also receive ministry from the persons whom they serve, whether or not they actually become church members.

—One urban church in a transitional neighborhood has established a food co-op, a used clothing center, a congregate meal program, a project for training severely handicapped persons and a community youth program. These are *signs* that the people called Christian in that place care about the people who live in the neighborhood.

—A suburban church has established an alternative school for youth who have problems adjusting to the routine educational program. It also developed an advocacy program to establish a community-based youth home for juvenile offenders. Here is a *sign* that a local church cares especially for youth often referred to as misfits.

—A community ministry developed a preschool program, an older persons' club, a youth recreation program, and a community development effort. This ministry was located in a public housing project, where unemployment, poverty, and crime were common. The ministry established a *sign* of care and concern, along with the preaching of the Kingdom.

—To reach people in need, a congregation in the center of a small, Southwestern city hired a social worker who coordinates the work of the service committee and thus enables members to support and participate in a variety of special community service initiatives (many of which are ecumenical). The congregation concentrates on meeting major gaps in existing public programs, and demonstrating new possibilities for service that empower relatively helpless groups.

—In addition to running a thrift shop and providing a "nest" for two Asian Christian fellowships, a small church in a large Midwestern city hosts an academy for high school dropouts and a language program for new immigrants. Both programs in this mainline congregation are staffed with the assistance of Mennonite volunteers.

—A holistic community ministry with an articulate biblical base is developing among black churches and poor communities in a rural section of a Southern state. This ministry features a cooperatively owned thrift shop, a health center, a music program, and a housing redevelopment corporation.

—In addition to these examples of community service, there are practical church initiatives to make public (food) assistance programs more effective through monitoring, outreach, emergency hotlines, gleaning, Meals on Wheels, etc.

4. As public funds for basic social services are reduced, it behooves the church to develop more competence in assessing social needs and fostering community programs. Take as a case in point the plight of the hungry. Much more is involved than being able to supply an occasional

bag of groceries. Not that the need for food banks will disappear. But the poor are entitled to something more, namely, advocacy of helpful policies and assistance in claiming public benefits to which they are entitled. A food pantry is *both* a window on the system of institutional injustice that increases hunger, *and* a limited way to plug large gaps in the public service delivery system. So a competent response goes beyond a bag of groceries.

In Southern California, church-related social service agencies have gone beyond providing emergency food only, to helping people also learn how to claim the social benefits to which they are entitled. As one social work coordinator described the evolution of this service: "We began by giving out bags of food. Then we added an interview and referral role. But we were still creating dependence, even though many congregations supported our direct services. The next step was to institutionalize the food pantry network with a nutritious three-day supply of food, coupled with expert help in getting emergency food stamps that very day. Then we began to ask how we could help prepare low-income people to deal with their problem more effectively. We still give out food, but we do many other things along with that." Symbolic of such increased competence in social service is a free newsprint publication by the Southern California Council of Churches, entitled *How to Get Food and Money: The People's Guide to Welfare and Other Services in Los Angeles County.*

Today, some members of congregations as well as area staff of the ecumenical denominations have considerable expertise in helping persons obtain federal food program benefits, general relief, aid for dependent children, health care, social security, legal aid, and employment opportunities. They can also monitor and influence the "regs" (the administrative regulations) that shape these programs locally, and in some cases have contracted with the public agencies to do "outreach" designed to make program benefits known to those who are eligible.

5. Competent Christian social service educates people for survival and self-development as much as it offers emergency aid. In the years ahead, more of both kinds of assistance will be needed: direct involvement with people who have urgent needs, and homework to keep up with changes in the social welfare establishment.

Competent social service can have an educational effect in predominantly middle-class congregations whose members are unaware that poverty and hunger are mostly caused by social biases, institutional barriers, arbitrary policies of government, low pay, inability to work, accidents or illness. Early results of the 1980 census indicate that more than one out of every three American households (27.2 million of the 79.1 million households counted in the 1980 census) used at least one of these five programs: food stamps, school lunches, public housing, Medicare, or Medicaid; and more than three quarters of those 27.2 million households were run by a woman, with no husband present. Some 215 million households lived in public or subsidized housing, with almost half of the households below the poverty line. Two thirds were run by women. A majority of the households were white. Consider the misery that has been induced by drastic cuts in public funding for these subsistence programs.

Meanwhile, the profile of older Americans has changed. In the 1980s almost 40 percent of the U.S. population over 65 will be black or first- and second-generation Americans belonging to various racial-ethnic subgroups. Compared to the majority of Americans, these minority groups are likely to have less education and money, substandard housing, poorer health, and shorter life spans—all of which make old age traumatic.

The urgency of social welfare ministry is obvious, as is the inadequacy of existing programs to meet many needs. The church can contribute to the redevelopment of competent social services by participating in service *with* people who have urgent needs, by doing homework to assess the extent of particular needs, and by learning how to utilize the available resources and to influence the existing policies of the social welfare establishment.

An Example: Empowering Services with Older Persons. Members of congregations, volunteers in community centers, students and teachers in seminaries and colleges can work together in an effort to comprehend how the social welfare system now serves or fails to serve marginalized groups such as the elderly. They will find helpful guides,[1] but no easy path, to community needs assessment. Resources to use in needs assessment include:

—Older persons who have particular needs and are familiar with the plight of their peers as deprived or serviced social rejects.

—Advocacy groups and community organizations such as the Gray Panthers, welfare rights organizations, older women's action networks, cooperative and shared housing groups.

—Traditional social welfare organizations such as United Way Information and Referral Service, Area Agency on Aging, the Social Security Administration, American Association of Retired Persons, the Department of Human Resources (Welfare), hospitals, nursing home administrators, local telephone hotlines.

—Census data (particularly from enumeration districts or block groups, if for a neighborhood), other public agency information from welfare department, planning office, schools, police, utilities; and resource files of universities, libraries, and newspapers.

—Reports of councils of churches; business, professional, and service organizations, and independent observers.

Summarize and interpret available information. Devote some time to "shaking out" your understanding of the most critical need(s), problem(s), issue(s). Write a concise summary of the needs to be met and most desirable methods of meeting them. Critique existing services and church ministries for older persons, identifying their strengths and weaknesses. Concentrate attention on developing patterns of relationships and forms of social organization which empower older persons:[2]

—To keep healthy and care for each other through community health services.
—To create shared intergenerational housing, exchange of services for upkeep and repairs, and community efforts to rehabilitate abandoned housing.
—To develop new options for work, bartering services, small local industries.
—To monitor pension policies and administration and provide reliable technical assistance on a low-cost basis for managing finances, retirements, etc.
—To form intergenerational teaching/learning communities; and educational programs sponsored by and for older persons.

Such an approach fosters self-reliance and mutual responsibility. It is a creative, caring alternative to expensive, bureaucratized public services produced by liberal government programs, and the enforced poverty and displacement which result from the conservative rollback of social programs and increased public subsidy for large private enterprise. Rather than perpetuate the society's paternalism toward the old, the church has a unique opportunity, through an empowering ministry with older persons, to give shape to a new age of responsible and enriching aging.

COMMUNITY ORGANIZATION—DEVELOPMENT

"Advocacy, interdependence, solidarity, life with and for others means not the exhibition of a private virtue of being helpful, or simply defining one's life as a helper. It means entering into the stream of life with all its systemic power arrangements, and swimming against that stream in a common struggle against oppressive powers which threaten the common life."[3] Advocacy is a matter of standing with powerless others, to plead their cause, to intercede, to espouse change.

The focus shifts *from* dealing with the individual effects of the social system *to* the methods of action that empower people to redevelop a community that knows liberation and justice. Attention also shifts from working *for* others to working *with* them in building awareness, resisting injustice, and organizing to gain the power and resources to be self-reliant and interdependent.

The community to be organized and developed is any social entity whose members share a common purpose, and which may include both a particular locality and a form of governance. "Community" may be a neighborhood, a city, a county, or a community of worshipers, workers, business people, or scholars. In fact, a whole approach to community organization works in several dimensions, and requires advocates or organizers who will intercede. (See diagram on the next page.)

The model highlights initiative in, and a flow between, all four sectors (or quadrants). The arrows suggest a cycle or spiral of response to a social condition, starting in any sector. The different aspects of community organizing are brought together in coalitions of groups concerned with the same or similar issue. Note that church members as well as community leaders are found along the whole length of the role axis, reflecting a continuum of leadership responsibilities and styles. Effective community organization in all four sectors requires continuous education and evaluation, as well as linking of private and public resources in coordinated action for change/ stability.

A whole strategy of community organization-development works on all four fronts when dealing with a major issue concern. The style of work, it should be noted, is both "bottom up" and "top down"; it assists those who now have limited access to power and it utilizes access to those who hold power. Allies in top-down action include the power elite, intervening elites, and leaders of interest groups.

AN INCLUSIVE MODEL: TYPES AND METHODS OF ORGANIZING FOR SOCIAL CHANGE/STABILITY[4]

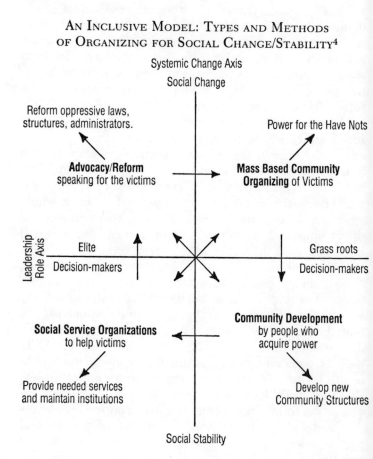

The bottom-up approach empowers people to form "a community of the sinned-against" who struggle against policies and institutions that are in the grasp of dehumanizing principalities and powers. Organizing of this kind begins with trustful listening and consciousness-raising. It recognizes that the victims of current policies and the advocates of reform are as "expert" about resolving their social problem as are the holders of political and economic power or the scholars who study the problem. Allies in the bottom-up process of action include leaders, researchers, and interpreters of low-power groups. Bottom-up organizing empowers a community to take charge of its own future. The purpose of such mass-based organizations is to build political strength and to coalesce institutional energy so that people can enjoy dignity and justice.

The issues that are chosen by this action process cross the left-right spectrum, seeking both change and stability, both shared resources and self-help. Today, many community organizations are talking about threats to the family from economic, community, and cultural pressures. (Given the 1980 census data mentioned above, perhaps this "issue" is not surprising.) The family has become a money machine that cannot keep up with stagflation (nor can churches, which are networks of families). The family experiences the corrosive effects of alcohol, drugs, pornography, and dangerous environments. The family experiences cultural pressure from television's violent and consumptive values, the local school's inept instruction and overscheduling, the demands and frustrations of work, etc.

How does a network of families, parish churches, and other allied groups gain leverage on this system? Each city has its own organizing stories to tell. Examples pertaining to family pressures can be far-ranging:

In Pittsburgh recently 200 parish leaders trekked through a blizzard to meet with area bankers. The residents were not carrying picket signs. They were carrying something much more powerful—institutional and family pledges to invest $5 million in a bank to be built in their community. The area needed a bank, and the bankers, when they understood the numbers of people and their dollars, saw that their self-interest lay in relocating a branch bank in their community.

In Los Angeles 3,000 Mexican-Americans from 24 parishes met to negotiate an agreement with an insurance company. The agreement stated that the company would provide favorable rates in exchange for a large volume of customers. The East Los Angeles organization had, in effect, created an insurance union and had the power to bargain for decent rates for car owners in their community.

In Chicago a parish that is part of a citizen's organization invited a local TV station to film drug transactions from a school window. The station agreed, and the activity was filmed. A special report was broadcast. The parish and organization then used this exposure to leverage a meeting with the superintendent of police, who under pressure, ordered a crackdown on narcotics traffic in that community.

These are some victories, the outward signs of institutionally based citizens' organizations, organizations which rearrange the relationship between families and churches on the one hand, and the major money and power institutions on the other. They recognize that power tends to come in two forms: organized people and organized money.[5]

Community organization enables people to face disruption, oppression, and inertia, and to exercise power to share a better future. Power is the ability to act; it has two key components: knowledge and constituency. "Knowledge and constituency offer a group power when the group has enough internal discipline to maintain a constant problem/issue/action methodology.... The most common misuses of knowledge and people (power) is the failure to be specific and establish a clear focus. A certain discipline is required for a group to sense and formulate a productive style of social action. The best method that we have found calls for moving from the problem to an issue and into an action. A problem is usually seen as a generalized concern, while the issue is a part of that problem seen as a handle that people can grab hold of and do something about. The action is what they do on that issue."[6]

This way of thinking, using energy as an example, can be diagrammed as follows:

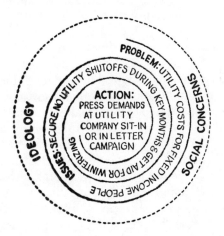

Community organization in the parish surrounding a congregation or group of churches will be effective to the extent that it identifies and acts on specific issues that grow out of urgent problems, and makes contact with key social forces and power structures that shape the community. It begins with simple *task-oriented* efforts to obtain better delivery of services; it moves toward *coalition-building* and *institution-forming*. In fact any significant community organization-development involves all three types of activity. It also utilizes the resources of community institutions and voluntary groups, bridges racial-ethnic divisions, and fosters alliances. The alliances may include secular organizations and clusters of churches.

Alert congregations can join or help to form community organizations of the kind described above. Participating congregations can also contribute directly to the identification of issues for concrete action, to gathering necessary resources for institution-building, and to fostering dialogue about common goals between organizations and powers in the community.

Every major community offers examples of organizing elite decision makers for purposes of community development. There is special work to be done with members of the ecumenical church's constituency who make up the economic, political, and cultural power structure. An example from Chicago is TRUST, Inc. (To Reshape Urban Systems Together), a small but influential catalyst for change. This organization, which was created by a pragmatic reformer named Janet Malone, conducts public forums and discussion groups on the assumption that the multiple crises of the cities are caused by ignorance, apathy, and hundreds of incremental decisions made in isolation with little regard for their overall impact. TRUST seeks balanced neighborhood investment, revitalization, and self-government, with special attention to cooperative housing and housing rehabilitation, support for small business, jobs for neighborhood improvement, better public services, and structures for local governance and development. A key target is to involve representatives from the affluent as well as impacted congregations, which can educate members about these problems, and give more focus to local benevolence giving.

Another example comes from Cleveland Heights, Ohio, where in the early 1970s, the Forest Hill United Presbyterian Church, facing the problem of resegregation of integrating communities, noted that housing stock was one key to stable integration. After a six-week seminar involving community leaders, real estate persons, minorities, and church leaders, and open to the public, the Board designed a program for housing rehabilitation based on a nonprofit housing corporation. The Forest Hill Church Housing Corporation was founded with a $5,000 grant from the Session, made possible with refinancing of the mortgage on the church building, freeing funds for mission. The Housing Corporation has grown to include leaders from the community and numerous churches and, through its Challenge Fund for low-interest loans to unbankable persons to rehabilitate their housing, has raised funds to insure $250,000 in loans.

At the same time, a local Catholic church was monitoring several real estate companies and discovering racist practices. From this study, Jewish, Protestant, and Catholic leaders formed the Heights Community Congress, a coalition of neighborhood, religious, civic, and business groups, whose goal was to promote an open, integrated community of the highest quality. Forest Hill Church joined this coalition and encouraged its pastor to serve as the president of the organization. This provided the church with full access to city government, neighborhoods, people of like-minded concerns, as a means of further enacting its commitment to reconciliation in society. Their efforts were informed by another congregation in Cleveland, Calvary United Presbyterian Church, which had already begun NOAH (Neighbors Organized for Action in Housing). With private and federal funds, NOAH has to date renovated or constructed housing for thousands of persons in a deteriorating area and generated similar housing efforts in other parts of Ohio.

These examples only begin to illustrate the multiple dimensions and complex dynamics of community organization-development. The examples show that planned social change involves coercion and consensus, a combination of massed people power and mobilized elites, technical know-how and voluntary talent, commitment to liberation and reconciliation as well as the gathering and application of resources to that end.[7]

Whether the church of the 1980s will recover a vigorous sense of public responsibility and express it in the ways just described is uncertain. Part of the miseducation of the clergy during the 1970s was precisely at the point of rendering congregational ministry more parochial—preoccupied with servicing the members and sticking to immediate in-church concerns. An indication of weakness is that much of the better literature on the church and community organization is over a decade old. But the sophistication about community ministry that can be found here and there in congregations is nevertheless a sign of hope that this mode of whole ministry in society will also be revitalized, as communities take charge of their future.

9

Engaging in Responsible Governance

A single action by Congress or one decision by the
President can undo—or multiply—many times over
the effect of all our voluntary contributions combined.
To make an offering in church for world relief and
quietly leave the big decisions up to political leaders
only encourages them to make *wrong* decisions. Our
silence is taken as indifference or hostility when
policies are hammered out, and hungry people become victims.

　　　　　—Arthur Simon, *Bread for the World*

High politics is *not* the art of the possible; it is the art
of enlarging what is possible and making what has
heretofore been impossible come in the range of what
can be considered.

　　　　　—William Lee Miller

The church is experiencing a crisis of public responsibility; its leaders are uncertain about the rationale, goals,
and methods of organized political engagement by people
of faith. Neither pastors nor members have been much
involved in public affairs and they seem to think it is
illegitimate for the church to do so. Meanwhile, the one or
two percent of church leaders who actually participate in
ecumenical legislative action networks feel a double mal-
aise: a sense of fruitless effort as they see hard-won policy
gains undone by reactionary holders of power, or a sense

of personal dissatisfaction with the mechanical procedures of letter-writing to public officials.

PUBLIC POLICY ACTION

A congregation undertakes responsible, winsome public policy action as:

—Public issues are explored openly in Christian education and expressed in the congregation's worship.
—Personal troubles are translated into public concerns that grow out of pastoral care and organizational know-how.
—Participants experience group support in this ministry.
—Congregations have timely opportunities for significant advocacy and dialogue with public officials, based on careful homework.
—Leaders offer a sound theological-ethical rationale for Christian participation in public affairs, and work for consistent social goals.

1. The first of these requirements was discussed in earlier chapters, so I will move directly to the second.

2. Legislative action can again be personalized. The connections are everywhere to be found on issues of sexuality, racial equality, economic justice, and national security. The public policy drama magnifies powerful personal fears: changing sex roles, ethnic pluralism, downward mobility, limited opportunity, or threatening nations with "alien" systems. Many people in our society are very anxious about what is happening to their family, neighborhood, job, living standard, and nation's prestige. They are tempted to follow leaders who offer simple answers and assign clear blame, while practicing constricting rather than generous forms of conservatism. Such leaders do translate personal troubles into public problems, but in demagogic, destructive ways.

The church's social preaching, teaching, and pastoral care can help people discern the unhealthy results of projecting their personal fears into the public arena and the consequences of ignoring the public sources of their "private" agonies. The objective is to work through social fear, anger, grief, and aggression to reach a point of communal creativity somewhere between apathy (whereby we ignore the issues) and anger (wherein we scream, claw, and scratch to get policies that satisfy psychic needs). The current problem, as Martin Marty quipped, is that "the civil people aren't committed and the committed people aren't civil. It's always easier to get people to rally around hate than around love. It's always easier to get a crusade going than an inquiry."[1]

Public policy involvement is a natural extension of pastoral care of members with personal problems that have social causes and effects. Our efforts to "help" can affect larger numbers of people when we not only care for individuals but seek to make changes in the social structures which will improve the quality of life.

Public policy involvement is both an outgrowth of ministry and a catalyst for ministry. This, sadly, is not the conventional wisdom. Sociological studies of church members reveal a standard thought pattern of either/or choice between "being oneself" or "helping others," "so that a person is forced to choose between personhood on the one hand and regard for the fate of one's neighbor on the other. From the perspective of the Pilgrim People of God, must not such a society be pathological?"[2] The askers of that question answer it with a careful analysis of Christians becoming "ethically mature." Research shows that persons who involve themselves in political activity *and* in the church are more likely to have a high level of satisfaction with friendship. "A person highly involved in politics and little involved in some form of 'public' religion is less likely to affirm friendship satisfaction and good health than the person who has both those former involvements. For the ethically mature, not only do 'religion and politics mix' but they mix with health and friendship in mutually fortifying ways." Moreover, because political involvement on behalf of social justice causes some anguish, participants need a supportive social group to sustain hope, to regenerate energy, and to maintain a sense of direction. "The reciprocal gift of such community is not less individuality but more. Friendships, church relationships, and political associations of the ethically mature seem to encourage them to combine assertions of their own personhood with sensitivity to other people."[3]

3. These findings underscore the need for supportive experiences of participation in public policy action that counteract feelings of complexity, irrelevance, or loneliness. It is not sufficient for legislative action workshops to brief people on the issues; at least as much time should be given to developing strategies of public policy action that enhance group support and broaden the base of local church involvement. Legislative action networks especially need pastoral care (an example of pastoral care of structures), lest they become mechanical and impersonal.

As for feelings of irrelevance, grass-roots letter writers are tempted to think that legislators or administrators are getting a lot of mail on the other side or have already made up their minds. Sometimes that is true, but more often legislators receive little significant mail and few phone calls from ordinary citizens, compared to the pressure from monied special interest lobbyists. Every thoughtful, concise communication makes a difference.

My awareness of this need to know whether our efforts are having an effect grew during the start-up years of the ecumenical hunger movement, when I chaired the governing board of the Interreligious Task Force on U.S. Food Policy, and conducted leadership development events for the Presbyterian Hunger Program. Time and again people would become attentive at even the mention of effective influence on issues of food aid, development assistance, farm policy, and domestic nutrition.

Still, to feel alone in this ministry is a natural commitment of the legislative action process. Pretty soon we begin to worry about being mere do-gooders. So it helps to gather in groups to review the very careful and practical legislative action material offered by the ecumenical networks, and to write letters together—i.e., to make the process a social experience.

A Clarifying Exercise. What have you done personally in the area of public policy in the last two or three years at federal, state, and local levels? Share the experience that was most significant or valuable to you. What made it such a memorable experience? What did you learn from it? And where did it lead you?

—Was this activity part of a network, or on your own?
—How was the church related to this public policy involvement?
—If it was a positive experience, did it involve supportive relationships? In the congregation? In the community?
—If it was a negative experience, can you explain why?

Sustained advocacy in public affairs depends on fellowship, identification of issue priorities, celebration of commitment, and periods of explicit theological reflection. These require face-to-face koinonia (participation). No amount of written, telephone, or cable communication will suffice to establish and nurture a supportive community for public policy action, though such communication certainly strengthens the effort. The community of support and dialogue is an important antidote to the trend toward manipulated publics which can be led on episodic crusades by purchasers of time on the electronic media. Our approach, instead, should be to undergird a life-style of ethical maturity which unites personal integrity and political action. This requires a different form of leadership and structure of organization than would be necessary simply to "turn on the troops." Legislative action coordinators must clarify their ambivalence at this point.

4. A fourth implication of the analysis is that the congregation can be led into responsible public policy action by a small group of persons who are willing to meet regularly and act wisely. This organizing group or committee needs to be clear about its ethical focus, timely in action goals, accurate with its factual information, creative in methods of influence. Specific tools are available for this work from ecumenical legislative action networks which alert members on what to communicate, when, to whom, and how on legislative issues.[4] Congregations that participate in these networks have a special opportunity to engage legislators in face-to-face dialogue, by visiting them and hosting their presence at community forums. As one congressman told me, "There is no substitute for eye contact with legislators and the staff to which they assign specific issues."

5. The people we want to involve in public policy action that has state and national impact also have local political concerns and can act in a variety of organized ways. A whole approach to politics that appeals to this ethically mature segment will not limit itself to legislative or administrative issues at federal and state levels. Public policy action also involves community education, mobilization, and coalitional action in cities and counties.

An Example: Public Action on Energy Responsibility. The mass media tend to focus on energy policy choices at the national and international level, with a heavy concern for increasing supplies in ways that serve the interests of government, corporations, and organized consumers. A macroanalysis of energy issues tends to create scale paralysis, though it occasionally translates into clear public policy action questions, such as whether to halt nuclear power plant licensing, to deregulate prices, to lease particular federal lands, etc. At the micro level—in terms of issues facing the local community—energy responsibility still includes these concerns, but there is more likely to be a diffuse politics concerned with the accountability of public utilities, siting and licensing of power facilities, aid to the poor and vulnerable facing rising fuel costs, opportunities to develop renewable energy systems at the community level. All of this is politics, and much of it can be very interpersonal, given the range of action methods available: hearings, demonstrations, public interest research, organizing for advocacy, behind-the-scenes negotiations, visits with public officials, media consultations, community development initiatives, energy fairs, work days, celebrative events, etc.

Public policy action, in short, is more than legislative; much politics goes on before, after, and despite legislation. Groups that make a coherent ethical appeal and present competent analysis are likely to influence policy discourse. The early stages of public policy action feature the work of preachers, teachers, and organizers who "inform" the politicians. (Thus the real originators of the 1964 Civil Rights Bill were not Lyndon Johnson and Everett Dirksen, but Martin Luther King, Jr., and many others in the civil rights movement who demonstrated, were beaten, jailed, and even killed.)

As for what happens after legislative action, the executive branch of government at every level also determines policy through regulations and administration of law. Church groups have had an important role in monitoring the administration of some legislation (e.g., food programs, international assistance, defense spending).

Many different associations and interests represented by people who are also church members come into play during the public policy process, and the interaction can produce common benefits. Not that tough problems will be "solved," since each solution creates new problems, but at least some problems will be engaged and social needs met.

Politics in this sense is a public service. It clarifies the social struggle to distribute scarce resources fairly and to exercise power responsibly for the common good. An appropriate Christian political posture is to *cooperate* with those who exercise power and those who struggle for power in ways that are responsive to human need and to *fight against* pretensions and injustices that arise when power endangers human welfare. Which brings me to the theological question of the church's political responsibility, summarized here in the light of my earlier writing and more recent experience.[5]

6. Some kinds of politics are irresponsible and good for neither church nor state, while other mixes of religion and politics serve the human household. The difference is evident in the following typology of responsible and irresponsible Christian involvement in politics:

ECUMENICAL SOCIAL CHRISTIANITY	NEW RIGHT CHRISTIANITY
GOAL	
Christians in politics with a vision of shalom.	Christian politics to promote public righteousness.
Help state be a better state.	Restore a theocratic order.
Seek the common good.	Seek religious-moral conformity.
STYLE	
Respect civil norms.	Crusading behavior.
Support religious and civil liberty.	Suppress nonconformists.
Multi-issue concern and action.	Narrow issue concentration.
Decriminalize sin.	Legislate against particular sins.
Appreciate religious pluralism.	Promote piety in public.
ETHICAL FOCUS	
Proximate justice informed by love.	Biblical directives for politics.

Righteousness as justice and peace.	Righteousness as purity and power.
Solidarity with oppressed.	Spiritual law and order.
Human liberation.	Individual liberty.
Cosmopolitan ethos.	Conventional morality.

Though the social policy truth is many-sided, responsible political behavior has a definite profile. The typology is a tool for analyzing how any group measures up in goal, style, and ethics.

Responsible Christian involvement in politics envisions better social arrangements which especially benefit the poor and vulnerable, and it advocates cosmopolitan justice. New Right Christianity, on the other hand, advocates freedom for those who already have considerable liberty and ignores the ways in which the present economic system oppresses the powerless.

Responsible Christian involvement in politics distinguishes between imperatives of faith and prevailing ideological assumptions. The New Right links Bible and flag, giving Christian sanction to national pride or greed.

Responsible Christian involvement in politics avoids a crusade against public officials who seek justice and appreciate complexity, but who are unorthodox on the issues. The New Right demands one view on selected issues, rating everyone accordingly, and punishing deviators at the polls (as did Prohibition-era Protestants).

Down the road, North American Christians may come together in broadening concern for economic and racial justice, in noncooperation with nuclear madness, in commitment to sexual equality and humanity, in efforts to assure everyone's right to a job, income, and housing, in programs of appropriate community and international development—just as half a century ago, Protestants abandoned the crusade for Prohibition and began to face issues of poverty, race, and war.

Meanwhile, churches and Christian groups that would be responsibly involved in public affairs will restrain their political rhetoric while doing prophetic inquiry, and foster qualitative analysis of issues as a basis for concrete action. The legislative information prepared by the ecumenical networks, such as IMPACT, Bread for the World, organizations of the Society of Friends, summarizes careful homework and makes ethical appeals that are designed to advance the public policy discourse of a pluralistic society. These organizations support networking, welcome coalitional action, and provide timely suggestions for action on national and state issues. No congregation can claim to have a whole ministry unless it participates in such networks, and in related forms of public policy action.

INSTITUTIONAL GOVERNANCE—CORPORATE RESPONSIBILITY

A ministry of governance is concerned with redirecting the resources and personnel of institutions to serve justice and peace. This mode explores the expression of social conscience in the governance of organizations, including the church, and clarifies the church's participation in corporate social responsibility. The goal is to be stewards of the public good in business, social service, and church structures. Through institutional governance, responsible selves shape social policy.

Biblical faith views patterns of governance, policy norms, and procedures of accountability as instrumental to the formation of a society consistent with God's liberating, reconciling freedom. Believers in the covenanting God seek to transform rather than to sanctify social, economic, and political institutions. Thus the prophets inveighed against unjust economics, and reasserted the spirit of Torah. Jesus condemned institutionalized greed (called Mammon), and called followers to a kingdom life-style. Revelation 13:11ff. challenged the emperor cult, a pseudoreligion designed to consolidate Rome's political and economic power,[6] and offered, in chs. 21 and 22, an alternative vision of the New Jerusalem.

How can the church today exhibit a parallel social and economic freedom? First, the church can change its own institutional practices in the direction of justice, stewardship, and community. Even routine decisions become theologically important: how to interpret, raise, and allocate the mission budget, how to utilize the building for social ministry, where to buy products and from whom to contract maintenance services (e.g., Project Equality), and what to expect of trustees in their management of property and investments.

Church officers—i.e., the ecclesiastical establishment—choose to use institutional assets in ways that more or less serve the surrounding community or enhance local/global justice. That such considerations often have to be shoehorned into the routine work of stewardship committees and the board of trustees is a clue to a perennial problem of institutional governance—how to reshape corporate policies in the direction of public responsibility. Sloth competes with greed to become the deadliest sin of every board of directors. The path of responsibility requires vigilant resistance against both forms of organized selfishness, and a willingness to venture into unfamiliar territory.

So corporate responsibility begins at home, but it does not end there. Members of the church often function as investors in, elected representatives to, or directors of business corporations, community institutions, service agencies, political parties, pension programs. In those settings, they are asked to endorse, if not debate, policies that have social consequence. In each decision there are many "stakeholders" who may or may not have their interests and claims represented. Henry Schacht, Chief Executive Officer of Cummins Engine Company, lists as their stakeholders: customers, suppliers, employees, creditors, distributors, communities, governments, publics, and, or course, shareholders. "We've come to the conclusion that acting responsibly has very little to do with what is now defined as public relations or public affairs. Rather it has to do with running the company. We have to acknowledge the multiplicity of demands, think about how we organize ourselves to meet those demands, and what our responsibility as managers really is."[7]

A Case Study.[8] A congregation hears a woman describe her torture in a South American country and her escape through the work of Christian folk in her native land and in the United States. Her arrest and torture was made possible by a computer system sold by XYZ Company to the police of her land.

The following week a church member who is a top computer sales representative for XYZ is told to go to another South American country to try to sell a computer to the police which could be used for the same repressive patterns. When he reports his concerns produced by the woman's description, he is told that a computer is morally neutral. XYZ cannot control how it is used.

He gathers a group of fellow church members to ponder what he might do. He knows that XYZ counts loyalty high in its individual performance ratings, that if he does not go, another salesperson will, that he has the right to protest the attempted sale clear to the top of the organization, but that such a protest may produce negative feelings toward him for rocking the boat. What should he do?

Split into small groups and discuss the various alternatives. Come back with a recommendation—i.e., what would you advise the sales representative to do about this dilemma? (This is still at the level of individual lay ministry.)

Then reconvene as the governing board (Session, Vestry, Official Board, etc.) of a local church to decide how to vote XYZ shares of stock on an ecumenical shareholders resolution developed by the Interfaith Center on Corporate Responsibility (ICCR). The shareholders' resolution requests information about computer sales to South American governments that may use such instruments for repression.

Assign various roles to these local church officers (Banker, Church and Society Chairperson, Employee of XYZ, Trustee of Presbytery/Diocese/District, Pastor, Leader of the Women's Association, Youth Group Representative, etc.).

—The Banker defends the bank's decision to invest in XYZ Corporation and other transnational corporations.

—The Church and Society Chairperson is eager to change church investment policies in the light of a one-year study of the impact of investments.

—The Employee of XYZ is painfully aware of the social limits of individual action, and would like the church to move corporately to raise questions about the morality of certain business practices.

—The Trustee of the regional church investment committee wants to maximize the income from church investments in high-yield stocks, while expressing social concern.

—The Pastor moderates the meeting and aims to please everybody.

—The Leader of the Women's Association has learned through participation in an ecumenical hunger-action program that some companies are marketing inappropriate products (e.g., infant formula) and others are developing agribusiness in poor countries at the expense of the local population.

—The Youth Group Representative has just taken a high school economics course in which she or he learned about Adam Smith's theories, but not about this.

Have the members of the governing board discuss the issue and offer a motion with regard to voting XYZ shares on the ICCR shareholder's resolution. Do *not* vote on the motion. Bring the proposal to an open congregational hearing. (Other participants can now raise questions and make comments.)

The case study exposes familiar tensions of individual conscience and institutional responsibility, and questions of whether and how the church should be a shareholder. The purpose of the church's corporate social responsibility strategy is to maximize the impact of being a stockholder group by evaluating the policies of corporate enterprises and filing disclosure resolutions, etc. It is not an attack on capitalism, but an approach designed to press corporations to fulfill their responsibilities to the larger public.

The Corporate Social Responsibility movement gained momentum in connection with civil rights and peace action, and soon encompassed environmental and women's concerns. Today the ecumenical effort, coordinated by the Interfaith Center on Corporate Responsibility, has working groups on Militarism, Community Reinvestment, Infant Formula, Agribusiness, Energy, Domestic Equality, Bank Loans, Labor Practices, Plant Closings, and the Role of Transnational Corporations. Coordination among churches and church agencies and other nonprofit organizations holding investment portfolios is beginning to develop; the church as shareholder is having an impact.

Meanwhile, persons involved in public relations and advertising divisions of the large transnational corporations have developed a counter-strategy to deal with their critics:

1. The critic is to be identified as an opponent of the system and thus discredited as a discussion partner.
2. Dubious motives need to be attributed to the critic: ideological or national prejudices, envy, stupidity, ignorance and lack of experience.
3. When criticism is global or circumstantial, the contrary is proved by means of isolated instances (e.g., description of an individual project).
4. When criticism is indisputable around a specific case

(e.g., in the case of ITT in Chile), emphasis is put on the fact that it is an individual case, moreover still under investigation.

5. ... Defending free enterprise is in everybody's interest. Therefore, it should be shown, especially in the mass media, that criticism of multinationals was basically criticism of free enterprise and that behind it were the enemies of the free world, whose view of life was based on Marxism.[9]

In their advertising, many transnational corporations now present themselves as friends of traditional values and as moral institutions with a family touch. Christians must be innocent as doves and wise as serpents in analyzing their work, and in focusing attention on the central question of corporate responsibility: What is the social result of each particular means of production and commerce?

While some segments of the business community are anxious to fend off any ethical critique of their policies and products, many Christians in the business community have come to recognize the church's responsibility as part owner in corporations to exercise diligently the rights of the investor, including options such as inquiry, correspondence, visitation, participation in meetings, buying or selling, and when appropriate, litigation. The most critical and extensive phase of work is a ministry of dialogue to explore the human-social effects of a given firm's policies and practices, and to seek changes of policy and practice for the common good. (The same logic and exercise of responsibility applies in the relationship between pension plan participants and those who administer a pension fund.)

The mission goal of the corporate responsibility movement is not to purify the motives of executives, directors, union leaders, trustees, nor simply to raise the question of individual vocation, but rather to explore the responsibility of each corporate entity. Since religious bodies in the

United States own about fifteen billion dollars in capital invested funds, and since the members of churches own many more dollars' worth of stock, the religious community's stake in corporate social responsibility is significant.

Historically, the Corporate Social Responsibility movement originated in a refusal to buy stocks in companies that produce liquor, tobacco, or arms. There is still a disinvestment dimension to the church's response, in withdrawing investments from military-industrial corporations that do a large volume of weapons-making, and in encouraging U.S.-based firms to divest their subsidiaries in or to withdraw their loans to countries controlled by repressive regimes. But for the most part it is a strategy of utilizing the investment as leverage to raise issues of corporate responsibility and to press for policy changes.

Related forms of action include: (1) *ministries of dialogue* with leaders of business and industry under auspices of industrial missions,[10] councils of churches, and local churches; (2) *campaigns of selective buying* (boycotts) to exert consumer pressure on unresponsive corporations (recent ecumenical boycotts focused on Nestlé Corporation, J. P. Stevens Company, and agribusiness firms that refused to bargain faithfully with the United Farm Workers); and (3) *creative investment* of endowment funds for the promotion of social goals (e.g., self-development enterprises, cooperatives for housing and renewable energy, and coalitions to mobilize community resources in the face of plant closings). In these ways also churches exercise economic stewardship, calling corporations and the public to account. An important example of creative investment is the Ecumenical Development Cooperative Society, which has several million dollars in investment funds from shareholder church groups on six continents whose purpose is to foster self-development enterprises.

In the local church a corporate responsibility strategy focuses on the economic responsibility of investors (including pensioners), trustees of endowed funds, leaders of institutions, executives of corporations. When dialogue and decision about the social effects of investments occur within a framework of Christian ethics and sound research utilizing basic corporate social responsibility publications,[11] the church can make a difference for economic justice.

Part III / CONCLUSION

10

Active Forms of the Church

The greatest need of our time is for koinonia, the call to simply be the church—to love one another, and to offer our life for the sake of the world. The creation of living, breathing, loving communities of faith at the local church level is the foundation of all the other answers. . . . It is the ongoing life of a community of faith that issues a basic challenge to the world as it is, and offers a visible and concrete alternative [when it is] the kind of community that gives substance to the claims of faith.

—Jim Wallis, *Sojourners*, 1980

Whole ministry in society is the responsibility of congregations, their governing associations, denominational bodies, and ecumenical agencies. Healthy congregations exhibit qualities of faithfulness in response to pressing social conditions and minister comprehensively through all available modes. Like the first congregations in exile, they are enjoined to "seek the welfare of the city where I [God] have sent you" (Jer. 29:7). And like the early Christians they share gifts in a common "ministry of reconciliation" as "ambassadors for Christ" commissioned to represent "the [justice] of God" (II Cor. 5:17–21).

A Unified Approach to Priority Concerns

Social ministry is more than the sum of particular issue responses; it is a unified, nonsequential way of worshiping, educating, caring, ministering on the job, acting for

183

community and institutional change, and influencing public policy. Having specified what can be done to redevelop each mode of congregational ministry, let me illustrate how the modes can be utilized in an integrated way over a period of time to respond to priority concerns.

This approach to social ministry emphasizes combinations of activity and quality of response. It does not require large congregations; the approach is scale-neutral. In fact, the following example summarizes the work of a congregation with less than one hundred fifty members over a period of four years.

An Example: Peacemaking Ministry Utilizing All the Modes. The Good Shepherd United Presbyterian Church in Commack, New York, has conducted a peacemaking ministry as follows:[1]

Preaching and Liturgy

—The regular Lord's Day worship of the congregation expresses the theme of peacemaking in a variety of ways: preaching from the lectionary provides opportunities to proclaim peacemaking and other social themes central to the Bible; the weekly "talk time with the young" often tells the story of "peacemakers" in history and in all walks of life; the choice of hymns avoids military images and emphasizes shalom and justice.

—Annual observance of Peace Sunday, sponsored by the Riverside Church Disarmament Project.

—World Communion Sunday offering for Peacemaking.

—Including those from other lands in invitations to preach; reflections by our own members who travel in other cultures.

—Use of *"Third World Sermon Notes"* in sermon preparation.

—Opening up liturgy, and prayers of the people to peacemaking concerns.

Pastoral Care

—The church is designated by its governing board as a Center for Draft Information and Counseling in the community, with the pastor and others trained to meet with young men and women, providing resources and counsel. In addition, each young man and woman in the congregation is invited to meet with the pastor to talk about his or her conscience formation in relation to war, peace, and the draft.

—Conversation and pastoral care with those who are employed in Long Island corporations with large military contracts, exploring values and conscience.

—Follow-up conversations after sermons that raise the issues of peacemaking, economic conversion, etc.

Education

—The congregation sponsored a mini-Riverside forum on disarmament, with *The Last Slide Show*, speaker, and discussion.

—The film *War Without Winners* was shown to the congregation on a Sunday morning.

—A Lenten study group of twelve persons gathered for six weeks to study women's program resource, "New Community for Peace."

—Continuing study of the biblical story of peacemaking, and of theologies of shalom.

—Four persons in congregation working on the "Nuclear Mapping Kit Project," showing effects of a nuclear bomb on Long Island. Members of church had helped to edit the kit when being drawn up by the American Friends Service Committee.

—Youth fellowship programs held on the draft, issues of war and peace, and hunger. Youth Retreat held a hunger simulation game, followed by 24-hour fast, with sponsored proceeds for Church World Service.

—Church officers are sent to continuing education events to develop peacemaking skills.

—Congregation provides leadership for presbytery workshops on peacemaking.

Lay Ministry

—Through educational programs and pastoral care and support, help is given the laity to exercise their ministry within the church, in occupations, and in voluntary service in the community and wider church.

—Conversations with church members working in the defense industry, in multinational corporations, etc.

Community Organization
—Involve members in Third World travel.

—Two of the church members are part of a Grumman Corporation Conversion Task Force, an informal *ecumenical* group carrying on talks with middle-management people about the goals of economic conversion and diversification for peacetime.

—Two community walk-a-thons were sponsored by our youth, to witness and raise funds (over $2,000) for Church World Service—emphasizing world economic justice.

—Members of our church were involved in developing community support for the Call to Halt the Nuclear Arms Race, serving as coordinators in our congressional district.

Social Service/Advocacy
—(See "Pastoral Care," above.) The church is a Center for Draft Information and Counseling in the community. As such we provide services for young men and women, and where necessary, advocate on their behalf, using the resources of the National Service Board for Religious Objectors.

—The church session also asked the Presbytery to establish draft counseling, which is being done through the Smith Haven Ministries, an ecumenical shopping mall social service ministry.

—Use conflict-resolution skills in community groups.

Legislative Influence and Public Policy Action
—The church belongs to several legislative information networks: American Friends Service Committee, in New York City, Bread for the World, national and state IMPACT, Interreligious Task Force on El Salvador, Riverside Church Disarmament Project, etc.

—Endorse nuclear "freeze," a proposal to halt and reverse the arms race.

—The Mission Committee of Session does research and writing on a variety of issues and places in the bulletin and congregational newsletter "Legislative Information Sheets" on issues before national, state, and local government. Several of these are regularly on peace and justice issues. Addressed envelopes are provided to appropriate legislators on each occasion.

—Church members are visiting our congressperson, presenting our views on the federal military budget and the cut in human services, out of a theological framework with a global concern.

—"Minutes for Mission" and announcements at worship frequently illuminate a peacemaking issue, showing the church's position and calling for study and action.

Institutional Governance

—Church members have shared peace education resources with local school officials, urging their inclusion in the school curriculum.

—The congregation supports disinvestment in nuclear warhead-making companies, and investment in Pax World Fund.

—Our members first drafted an Overture on Peacemaking sent by Presbytery to the 1980 General Assembly.

—The congregation participates in a denomination-wide Institutional Life-style Change Project in which we seek to make connections between our church's lifestyle and world economic justice and peace issues.

Several basic characteristics of a unified approach to social ministry are evident in the illustration.

1. The modes of ministry are developed in combination, rather than in sequence. Activity occurs in several modes simultaneously, though there may be concentration on a few of them at a time. A key to this approach is to combine both in-parish modes (such as preaching and liturgy, pastoral care, education) and community-oriented modes (such as lay ministry, community organization, social service/advocacy, public policy action, and institu-

tional governance). A whole social ministry does not develop if there is a preoccupation with only one set of modes. (One implication for leadership development is to develop individual competence in both kinds of modes so that preachers have experience in public policy action, liturgists and counselors know something about community organization, lay ministry links with institutional governance, education encompasses social service/advocacy concerns—to show but a few possible combinations).

2. A whole strategy does *not* require that every mode receive equal attention, nor is it helpful to worry about whether a particular activity has been classified under the correct mode. Ministry in some of the modes may occur by supporting or reorienting existing work of other community or church organizations, rather than initiating new work in each mode. The modes also overlap, so that some activities involve more than one mode. The point of the analysis is to comprehend the rich combinations of activity and the quality of response that comprise a whole ministry. Each mode of ministry can be developed at several levels of complexity or depth.

3. Congregations that exhibit quality social ministry stay with major areas of concern for years, being careful to develop their ministry within a coherent social-ethical analysis. They become adept at redefining the issues within these broad concerns, and they learn to work imaginatively in various modes of ministry so that their approach is both pertinent and winsome.

The above example outlines multi-mode ministry on one priority concern. But it should not be read to mean that multi-mode ministry concentrates exclusively on a single issue. Whole ministry expresses theological discipline in ways that are both multi-issue and multi-mode. Good Shepherd Church, like other lively congregations in social ministry, responds to more than one concern at a time, but "majors" in a few—no more than three—social concerns. The other majors of the Commack, New York, congregation are hunger action and equal rights for women. Members of the congregation also "minor" in other issues which only involve the whole congregation peripherally or episodically. Thus, a few members and the pastor of Good Shepherd Church participated in advocacy efforts to establish a hostel-residence home for discharged mental patients from the state hospital, but they did not develop this into a major congregational concern. Over time, of course, a minor can become a major, and vice-versa, since issues change. Major areas of concern, however, remain relatively constant.

4. This approach, with all the modes in mind, is a way to plan, implement, and evaluate a quality social ministry. Such a ministry has *breadth* as it encompasses the various modes. A multi-mode analysis of current activity helps to correct any tendency to narrow down to a couple of modes. Such a ministry has *depth* to the extent that each mode is carefully understood and developed. The quality of each mode of ministry depends on the combined creativity, insight, and gifts of church members as they affirm God's justice-love, leaven social institutions, and work with others of humane purpose for the common good.

This unified approach fits the experience and stimulates the imagination of socially concerned parish leaders who may not have been using these terms, but who recognize that sustained ministry on any major social concern develops through a dynamic combination of priestly, pastoral, prophetic, and political activity. Thinking in terms of the modes gives more specificity to this way of doing ministry.

5. It should be obvious that multi-mode social ministry is done by congregations, and not only their professional staff. The vision and skills of pastors and other professional church workers are crucial to the leadership of this ministry of the people. Professional church workers who are insecure or myopic certainly can exercise veto power and block the development of this ministry. But a positive development of it depends on the congregation's commit-

ment to minister in a whole way with the competent involvement of the laity.

Finally, this approach assumes that there is only one ministry which is thoroughly social in ways that encompass the personal and the political, the prophetic and the pastoral, the active and the educational. False polarities are bridged in an integrated way that permeates the church milieu and affects the social ecology. The ecological analogy is pertinent, since we know that small changes in ecosystems and human habitats can have far-reaching qualitative effects in terms of destruction or health. The same goes for the development of ministry. A whole approach to social ministry assumes that all modes or dimensions of ministry have social significance, and must be developed with care and competence.

This approach to social ministry pertains to *any* major concerns a congregation or larger church body may have. The strategy is to act on priority concerns in a whole way utilizing all the modes. Space does not permit me to include additional examples of multi-mode ministry in response to issues of employment, housing, education, land use, food policy, changing family, drug abuse, the crisis in human services, etc.[2]

Choosing Issue Priorities

I asked the pastor of Good Shepherd Church, which supplied the example of peacemaking ministry, to collect all "cause" mail for a few months. During that time he received 228 different items from 106 different groups. Stapled together, these items stretched across a meeting room several times, making quite a "laundry list." He also kept track of the concerns of his presbytery's Public Issues Committee, which, within a year, had a laundry list of more than two dozen issues arising from national developments, denominational emphases, organized networks, voluntary organizations, local controversies, and the pet concerns of committee members. Were they choosing the issues or were the issues choosing them? And could they do anything about so many issues, other than talk briefly about each?

How do we sort out the list and determine priority concerns that can receive sustained attention in a whole strategy of ministry? Actually in most congregations a few members with particular interests, involvements, and talents convince at least some group in the congregation to concentrate on their concerns for a time. That is a natural political process in voluntary groups. But how can churches deal more effectively with the laundry list of issues and act on the most important social concerns?

Criteria for selecting a priority social concern are the following:

> Serious and pervasive condition
> Demands Christian ethical attention
> Neglected by powers and authorities
> Most urgent to poor and vulnerable
> Also middle-class interest
> An opportunity for empowerment
> Arouses broad community concern
> Has both global and local dimensions
> Has concrete and manageable handles
> A denominational or ecumenical priority
> Chance to make a systemic difference
>   as well as to meet a service need
> Will elicit resources of the congregation:
>   Talent, Money, Leaders' Support, Members'
>   Energy
> Available modes for response

Any neighborhood-parish, country-regional, or national-international issue that meets most of these criteria may become a priority concern for congregational ministry. Significant social ministry responds to public issues or conditions that

—Demand attention in the light of Christian ethical vision and values.

—Are important and actionable locally (but are more than parochial).

—Fit into an overall strategy of the congregation and regional judicatory, or its ecumenical association.

—Elicit local energy and resources—persons, organizations, funds.

Planning for priority action utilizes the resources of councils of churches, metropolitan or county agencies, social justice programs, specialized ministries, as well as census data and knowledgeable sources in public agencies. Strategic action planning should also bring to bear the insights gained from periodic community studies and public meetings that expose conditions requiring urgent attention.

When priorities are selected, the next strategic steps are to set goals and to develop a plan of action—a subject treated in available literature and a skill of action-training consultants.[3] When developing a strategic action plan, keep in mind that multiple modes of ministry are available, and that these methods of action should be utilized in a theological-ethical framework which orients the congregation's response to priority social concerns.

Ministering Members

Form follows function. Whole forms of the church emerge as *members* participate in mission/ministry. An overseas example of immediate significance are the *base communities* (comunidades de base) that emerged in Latin America, Holland, and Italy under the influence of liberation theology. The significance of these Basic Christian Communities is in their whole life as communities of people whose worship, education, pastoral care, and public engagement includes cultural, economic, and political concerns. Basic Christian Communities seek to unite biblical-theological reflection with social analysis leading to action in the world. Members support one another in striving for justice and offering abundant community for all.

> The base community as I perceive it serves two basic functions: it provides outreach for social transformation, and it provides a vehicle for effective evangelism. These functions occur because the base community has a self-image radically different from the usual self-images of small groups in North American churches. The base community understands itself to be the church in action, not deferring to other persons, groups, times, or places the responsibility for ministering. Small groups in North American churches defer generally to the congregation and its official leadership. Persons encountered and befriended are steered to committees and classes and task forces, and the small-group member returns to the private interests of the small group, be it Bible study, prayer, or quilting. The base community views itself to be the church wherever it is and in the face of whatever challenge it meets. Although it is the church, it is *not* all that there is of the church, and the base community in turn brings its converts and its projects to the whole congregation to which it is accountable.[4]

There are some North American parallels or adaptations of this church form, where each member of the congregation is expected to join a studying, praying, sharing, ministering group that meets weekly. Some congregations organize themselves into intergenerational mission groups (small enough to meet in a house), which may be called apostle groups, service teams, or advocacy groups (the label usually connotes a particular way of working). This *base community* form, adapted to different settings and emphases, is the missing link between the *corporate church* with its formal structure and institutional caution, and *concerned individuals* who need organizational and personal support to stay in faithful ministry.

A related organizational form that is especially appropriate to larger congregations and that forges the missing link between concerned individuals and corporate structures or official committees of the congregation is the *advocacy group*. This mechanism allows action-minded members of a congregation to minister freely in response to social concerns. As developed by the (United Presbyterian) Community Church in Davis, California, the advocacy policy enables individual members to be informed and encourages them to get together in inquiry/action group(s) in the congregation or ecumenically. The group(s) exist for "action." The governing board of the congregation endorses this style of involvement and is receptive to the advocacy of individuals and groups outside the church who want to gain church support for liberating, reconciling action in society. The following guidelines govern the application of the Advocacy Policy:

1. Any two or more members of the congregation may join together in an Inquiry/Action group to work in behalf of a particular cause, project, candidate which they consider to be in furtherance of the will of God. Recognition of Inquiry/Action groups is delegated to the Church and Society Commission of the Session. Such groups will be guided by the following principles:

a. They may not use the name of the congregation, denomination, or session. They speak in behalf of their actual members only.

b. Membership of such groups is available to the Session on request.

c. Inquiry/Action groups may use the church bulletin boards, mailing lists, mimeograph machine, space in church newspaper within reasonable limits. Session reserves the right to determine what is "within reason."

d. Inquiry/Action groups may be related to or include groups from other churches—Presbyterian or ecumenical—and secular groups similarly concerned.

e. The minister and other staff may work with groups as concern leads them. The minister shall provide minimal staff service to any groups requesting it.

f. Session may on occasion feel an Inquiry/Action group to be diametrically opposed to its understandings of the gospel as interpreted by the confession of the church.

g. Existence of the Inquiry/Action groups shall in no way preclude the duty and right of the Session to declare its conscience on any matter of doctrine or conduct.

2. The Davis Community Church will be receptive to individuals and Inquiry/Action groups from outside the church membership seeking the participation and the support of the church members in some cause but in this instance permission to sponsor a meeting, distribute information, or circulate a petition must be granted by Session (unless the Session specifically acts to endorse the cause), and no judgment is intended or implied toward those who differ from the position being taken.

3. Though the initiative in the Advocacy Policy rests with the advocates themselves, the Session will endeavor to create a climate where freedom is given to the advocates of all sides of a particular issue to be represented.

The Advocacy Policy does not allow for events sponsored by a particular political party or for the promotion of a particular political candidate. It does, however, allow for bipartisan or nonpartisan discussion of candidates.

4. Inquiry/Action groups will be given space on a limited time basis only. Permission granted once does not guarantee permission for other activities by the same group.

5. No activity permitted under this policy shall be closed or secret. Public notice of each event shall be given and interested people may attend.

6. Session reserves the right to review and limit any actions it deems inappropriate.

This form of the church creates a climate of expectation for faithful social education and action and welcomes the gift of prophecy, while recognizing that other members of the congregation have different inclinations or gifts. The pastors of the congregation invite the advocacy groups to share their concerns through mission announcements and prayers of the people. The pastor's own role is "to inspire, support, encourage, and join with the minority that is socially active, and at the same time appeal to the majority from the standpoint of the gospel, in order to 'convert' some of them to the activist position of the minority, and in the case of others, to act, at the very least, to encourage tolerance of the ministry which the minority is carrying out in the congregation and the community."

An advocacy policy establishes a new consensus about the public ministry of church members, even as it recognizes the reality of multiple constituencies in the congregation—the socially apathetic, defenders of the status quo, and advocates of social justice and peace. A congregation with advocacy groups expands the audience for, and broadens participation in, while reducing entrenched opposition to, social engagement. Members have concrete action opportunities and organizational support undiluted by the demand that everyone agree first. Even those who joined the church primarily to be assured of their well-being, and hoped at minimum cost to receive blessing for their current way of life, can be enlisted in new expressions of faithfulness.

Contours of Socially Involved Congregations

In 1969–70, a colleague and I studied a set of 105 Most Socially Involved Congregations (MSIC's)[5] which were chosen on the basis of quantitative criteria: (1) the number of different social issues engaged by the congregation, (2) the total number of activities reported: e.g., formed a permanent committee, a temporary task group, prepared a written report, or undertook an action program, and (3) the frequency of combined activities coupling either a "written report" or an "action program." Congregations whose annual report showed at least twelve activities on at least six different issues, and three or more combinations of organization and action were classified as "*most* socially involved." These congregations were of all sizes, though predominantly white, *large* congregations were overrepresented at three times their denominational proportion, while small congregations (under 250 members) were underrepresented in almost the same proportions. Even so, 45 percent of the most involved congregations had less than 500 members, and nearly half of these were predominantly nonwhite. Thus the colorful (and bicultural) congregations were much more likely to be socially active. Conversely, predominantly white congregations with less than 500 members were least represented among the MSIC's, suggesting that special steps must be taken with these congregations to overcome racial and cultural isolation.

There was no clear relationship between social involvement reported by a congregation and its institutional decline or growth. We determined this by comparing the MSIC's with a cross-sectional sample of congregations in the denomination. During the previous five years, a slightly higher percentage (47.6 percent) of the MSIC's gained members than did the congregations in the cross-sectional sample (45.4 percent). But the MSIC's showed a higher net loss, probably because larger congregations, when declining, tend to have a larger net loss of numbers and percent of members. At any rate, the membership growth and decline picture is quite inconclusive. The same was true of mission giving, with *less* decline in mission giving among the MSIC's.

As for their priority concerns, both the small, central city, predominantly black MSIC's and the large, suburban, white MSIC's tended to concentrate on felt needs where they were and were reluctant to tackle issues that did not seem close to them. Both kinds of congregations tended to be constructively adaptive in their immediate locale. If this involvement reflected considerable concern for the welfare of the parish, it did not often make global connections.

The congregation's social setting, awareness of issues, previous experience, financial resources, are all situational factors that affect involvement. Their shared sense of mission priorities, social goals, organizational know-how, and skills in coping with conflict are leadership factors that enhance social ministry.

While the above data and comments suggest the promise of larger congregations, one should not thereby conclude that larger congregations are making unusually effective use of their resources—members, staff, budget—for purposes of social engagement. As one elder put it for several we interviewed, "The congregation isn't involved, just small segments of it." How larger congregations can fulfill their capability, given their resources, is a subject deserving special study.

A decade later, *in 1979–80,* I administered an institutional life-style change project involving forty Presbyterian congregations whose sessions covenanted to change their own and the congregation's life-style in the direction of justice, stewardship, and community. This time smaller congregations were represented, or declared themselves as participants, in proportions roughly opposite from the 1969 study. Our field exploration focused on the *quality* of congregational life and leadership rather than the quantity of socially responsible activity (though these are reinforcing characteristics in a whole social ministry). The following generalizations are based on my conversations with representatives of some "covenant" congregations, and on the observations of the part-time project coordinator who visited many of these congregations.[6]

Justice-oriented congregations are "in touch" with others. They share awareness of the embodied needs of people and express a strong sense of responsibility for social mission. The theme is always there, like a *cantus firmus* in a Bach chorale. In worship, the people celebrate this mission and expect to hear of fresh instances in which the congregation is taking sides for liberation and reconciliation.

These congregations have a social ministry lore, which includes interest in the history and tradition of whole, public ministry. The lore is repeated in connection with Christian education, in their social interpretation of Scripture during worship, in meetings of the officers, and in celebrative events.

At their best, these congregations concentrate on a few—one to three—emphases, or major social concerns, at a time. The priority concerns permeate all dimensions of congregational life, and utilize multiple modes of ministry. Participants exhibit widespread understanding of corporate as well as personal dimensions of justice issues, and they tend to think globally as well as to act locally.

Recognizing the contradictions in which they exist as relatively affluent North Americans, justice-oriented congregations are concerned about more appropriate use of resources, including the church building, budget, and staff time for the sake of faithful witness in society. At the same time they celebrate their community in shared meals, prayer, study/action, fellowship. These congregations exhibit innovation in worship, intergenerational participation, serious adult study, shared leadership, and a willingness to take risks with their resources. In these congregations, as in socially active congregations of the earlier study, "strong" pastoral leadership and vocal lay support are crucial. It is a leadership style that takes and delegates responsibility, making use of the members' gifts as well as the resources of the surrounding community and the larger church.

Justice-oriented congregations encourage the members to be socially involved, and try to keep internal church structure simple enough to enhance personal fellowship and external engagement. The congregations' leaders plan carefully, but flexibly, for the common ministry of clergy and laity.

Social Ministry and Church Health

The positive relationship between whole ministry and church health deserves more attention in an era of anxiety about declining membership. Healthy churches are socially involved—showing compassion, doing justice. In fact, we can add another stereotyped either/or (either significant social ministry or healthy church growth) to the scrap heap of false dichotomies. "Growing mainline congregations are significantly more involved in community activities, and community groups are significantly more likely to be using church facilities. Further, the members of growing mainline churches indicate that they derive satisfaction from churches which include a strong social ministry."[7]

But many church leaders and members still (wrongly) assume that social involvement and congregational diversity are major causes of declining membership, and are tempted to accept idolatrous schemes of church growth that foster homogeneous groupings geared to meeting people's religious needs in privatized ways. The idea is to "make disciples" by proclaiming a message that would satisfy personal needs while "postponing ethical awareness" for a later "perfecting" process. As if Jesus had commissioned his disciples to "baptize them as soon as possible, but wait quite a while to teach them all I have commanded you" (see Matt. 28:19–20). This philosophy of church growth welcomes homogeneous groupings segregated by race and class, in disregard for the heterogeneous Christianity of Acts and the Pauline epistles. It proposes eventually to explore "ethical issues such as learning to live in peace and harmony with those of other homogeneous units,"[8] but considerations of faithfulness are not to be confused with the growth business of the church.

Given such idolatrous religious enterprise, it is important to reassert qualitative over quantitative considerations, and to speak of church health more than of church growth in connection with whole ministry. What exactly are the positive connections between social ministry and church health? Careful studies suggest the following generalizations:

1. Socially involved congregations are healthier than those which insulate themselves from social involvement.

Comparisons between congregations that are demographically similar indicate that social ministry actually strengthens the institution. Mainline congregations that meet social service needs and advocate social justice tend to have more members and supporters. In situations of member flight, community involvement at least ameliorates institutional decline and sets the stage for congregational redevelopment to meet human-social needs and to include residents of the immediate parish.

2. Socially involved congregations do not necessarily grow or decline faster than others. "Church membership growth is largely situational: where the church is located is more important than what the church does."[9] Quantitative growth or decline is affected by demographic change and community compatibility, as well as the affinity between dearly held values of the members and priorities of the congregation's leaders. As one pastor of a new church development in a booming Southwestern city put it, "We open the doors and they come in; I shouldn't take credit for that kind of growth."

3. Healthy-minded people are attracted to churches that integrate horizontal and vertical beliefs and that seek to be relevant to societal and community issues. This is an especially prominent interest of the natural constituency of the ecumenical denominations, which "have a distinctive contribution to make as they join the warm heart to the clear head and busy hands. Their mission is to present the claims of the Christian faith to those who have been most impressed by the empirical approach of the sciences or by those critical social needs which call for rapid and thoroughgoing change. This constituency includes ... many humanitarians seriously hoping for basic improvement in our social situation and convinced that churches in general are either benighted or inactive concerning such matters."[10]

4. Church membership trends as a whole are unaffected by church social involvement. Just as membership decline has not generally resulted from social involvement, mem-

bership growth will not be a direct payoff of social ministry.

> People who are contacted by the social involvement of the church are not more likely, or less likely, to join the membership of the congregation. In fact, many people who participate actively in the community ministries of the church are not members of the congregation. Many congregations with community programs have discovered a large constituent group, the "friends of the church," who support its ministries without belonging to the church. Apparently the strength and growth of church membership is a rather indirect consequence of community programs.[11]

5. Congregations that are growing in numbers and commitment of members are more likely to be socially involved to the extent that members have enthusiasm for specific priorities of social ministry and have confidence in their leadership. Confidence in leaders depends on both style and substance. Clergy and lay leaders must be trustworthy in leadership methods and credibly grounded in biblical theology as they foster social ministry.

6. Church leaders and members may divide over methods of social ministry. Social action that is critical of the status quo can inhibit congregational growth. Social service programs can accelerate congregational growth. Some forms of involvement in "radical" social action have resulted in lay persons' reaction and withdrawal of support, but "people often *join* the church or *increase* their financial support *because* they see religion being relevant to societal and community issues."[12]

7. "Interpersonal differences regarding social action are very important in the growth or decline of some congregations."[13] Some forms of social action can be detrimental to congregational cohesion where commitment is already low or faith priorities are unclear. Across the church in congregations generally, members are wary of social activism that pushes hard either to the left or to the right. In the '60s a radical left, as perceived through mass media

reports, aroused suspicion. Now in an era of radically reactionary politics allied with Fundamentalist religion, there will be more dispute about the appropriate social roles of the church. A careful look at the qualities and comprehensive character of whole ministry in society should enable participants to work through this conflict.

8. A healthy, sometimes growing church is a gift to be appreciated and utilized for mission. But we really do not know how it happens. Healthy church life and growth in membership is a mystery beyond the reach of organizational management or the findings of empirical research. The literature on church growth has singled out several local institutional factors that were presumed to be crucial. It turns out, however, that "theological tendencies, priority given to evangelism, desire for growth, and compatibility of pastor and laity are *not* important causes" of church growth.[14]

What, then, do we conclude about the relationship between social involvement and church health? We can affirm, on grounds of theology and experience, that a healthy church engages society, that it does so qualitatively and comprehensively, and that its members and leaders have a shared consensus about the social significance of being people "in but not of the world," who clearly understand, warmly share, openly practice faithfulness.

Social-Psychological Competence in Conflict Situations

Recognizing that involvement in public affairs is a lightning rod for conflict in the church, social ministry leaders should learn what to do before conflict intensifies and how to act during conflict.[15]

To Prepare for Conflict

1. Recognize its normalcy in the process of adjusting to new realities and in the process of growth.
2. Develop an understanding of the church in the world as an always sinful sign of the Kingdom (in Augustine's words, the city of God and the city of Man commingle until the end of history).

3. Foster a comprehensive, quality program of social ministry, with options for individual involvement.
4. Build an expectation of reconciliation as a result of conflict over specific social issues and methods of ministry.
5. Utilize democratic procedures; respect minority positions.
6. Nurture loving relationships and mature, emotionally healthy individuals.

During Conflict

1. Act promptly to demonstrate commitment to the above points.
2. Emphasize consensus on overall goals, based on commonly accepted Christian values.
3. Present challenging ideas in a context of personal acceptance. A + C = G. Acceptance plus confrontation equals growth.
4. Establish a fair procedure for conflict resolution.
5. Use an outside facilitator or consultant in deteriorated situations.
6. Maintain a problem-solving approach with a data base ("What is best for all of us?").
7. Communicate the facts straightforwardly about controversial decisions and how they were made.
8. Spend time with people who disagree.
9. Propose creative solutions (e.g., compromise, integration, pluralism).
10. Specify agreements and plan next steps.

These principles of conflict resolution do not work where hierarchical power is exerted or where parties to the conflict refuse to play fair. But when fairly applied, they often work to keep conflict constructive.

Supportive Structures

Far from being unmanageable, uneconomic, or impractical, whole ministry in society contributes to personal fulfillment, congregational renewal, community well-being, and ecumenical integrity. As this new ecology of social ministry is practiced in congregations, interpreted in the gatherings of larger church bodies, and taught in continuing education, old stereotypes of social involvement will be displaced by coordinated support for a whole approach.

Once we comprehend that all ministry is social and that every unit of the church has responsibility for it, the special obligation of the church's regional and national judicatories and agencies is:

—To field staff with skill in social ministry and resources to develop it.

—To foster theologically disciplined continuing education of clergy and laity to equip congregations for whole ministry in society.

—To influence church decision-making, mission planning, and allocation of budgets to enhance social ministry in congregations and connectionally among them.

—To develop ecumenical mechanisms for planning and implementing ministry in specialized sectors, in areas of cities or counties, and through particular programs of social justice.

With reference to each of the four support responsibilities listed above, there are established barriers to overcome in the larger church. Overextended staff need permission and assistance to reexamine current practice, to identify fresh resources, and to work with more competent groups for a revitalized ministry in society. Theological and continuing education centers are tempted merely to add a course to the smorgasbord of fragmented specialities, rather than to redesign learning opportunities within a coherent theory of ministry. Key church decision makers, anxious about maintaining smoothly functioning institutions in times of inflationary pressure and troubling social change, still remain anxious about "too much social involvement." And a decade of reduced ecumenical initiative leaves us relatively unprepared to foster fresh ministry in society's key sectors to express priority social concerns.

But these same leaders, along with many local pastors and members, are quite capable of doing a new thing—to undertake a whole social ministry which derives from biblical faith, encompasses personal needs, contributes to the public good, and revitalizes congregational life by being active for freedom, justice, and peace in a broken world.

Notes

Preface

1. Resources for social ministry leadership development, including a looseleaf notebook for participants, are available from the Program Agency, The United Presbyterian Church U.S.A., Room 1101, 475 Riverside Drive, New York, N.Y. 10115

Chapter 1. To Reconstruct a Whole Ministry

1. Harold Quinley, *The Prophetic Clergy: Social Activism Among Protestant Ministers* (John Wiley & Sons, 1974), p. 140.

2. Yoshio Fukuyama, *The Ministry in Transition: A Case Study of Theological Education* (Pennsylvania State University Press, 1972), p. 95.

3. Dieter T. Hessel, *Reconciliation and Conflict: Church Controversy Over Social Involvement* (Westminster Press, 1969), Ch. VI, "When Church Bodies 'Pronounce.'"

4. Henri Nouwen, *Creative Ministry* (Doubleday & Co., 1976), p. 79.

5. Ibid., p. 70, and p. 119.

6. My profile of the two-party system is informed by firsthand experience in ecclesiastical politics, and by Martin E. Marty, *Righteous Empire: The Protestant Experience in America* (Dial Press, 1970), Ch. 17; and Neil Q. Hamilton, *Recovery of the Protestant Adventure* (Seabury Press, 1981), Part I.

7. David A. Roozen and Jackson W. Carroll, "Recent

Trends in Church Membership and Participation," in Dean R. Hoge and David A. Roozen, eds., *Understanding Church Growth and Decline, 1950–1978* (Pilgrim Press, 1979), p. 37.

8. Dean R. Hoge, *Division in the Protestant House: The Basic Reasons Behind Intra-Church Conflicts* (Westminster Press, 1976), p. 87.

9. Dean Hoge and David Roozen, eds., "The Unchurched American," *Review of Religious Research*, Vol. 21, No. 4 (Supplement 1980), esp. pp. 391, 469.

10. Roy I. Sano, "A Cosmopolitan Ministry," in Dieter T. Hessel, ed., *Rethinking Social Ministry* (The Program Agency, The United Presbyterian Church U.S.A., 1980), p. 64.

11. Donald W. Shriver, Jr., and Karl A. Ostrom, *Is There Hope for the City?* (Biblical Perspectives on Current Issues) (Westminster Press, 1977), p. 109, and Ch. 5.

12. Wes Michaelson, "Shaping Social Welfare Mission in the '80s," *Church and Society*, March-April 1979, pp. 47–48.

Chapter 2. EVERY CONGREGATION'S DILEMMA

1. Michaelson, "Shaping Social Welfare Mission in the '80s," p. 48.

2. Gabriel Fackre, *The Christian Story* (Wm. B. Eerdmans Publishing Co., 1978), p. 160.

3. Adolf Harnack, "The Gospel of Love and Charity," in *The Mission and Expansion of Christianity in the First Three Centuries*, tr. and ed. by James Moffatt (Peter Smith, 1972), pp. 147–198.

4. James D. Davidson et al., "Increasing Church Involvement in Social Concerns," *Review of Religious Research*, Vol. 20 (Summer 1979), pp. 291–296.

5. Ibid.

6. Kenneth Underwood, *The Church, the University, and Social Policy*, Vol. I (Wesleyan University Press, 1970), p. 7.

7. Ibid., p. 431.

8. Ibid., p. 75.

9. Ibid., p. 391–397.

10. Ibid., p. 100.

11. Ibid., pp. 230–231.

12. Ibid., pp. 294–295.

13. Fukuyama, *The Ministry in Transition*, pp. 97–98.

14. Ibid., p. 15.

15. James D. Anderson and Ezra Earl Jones, *The Management of Ministry* (Harper & Row, 1978), p. 113.

16. Quinley, *The Prophetic Clergy*, p. 303.

17. John C. Harris, *Stress, Power and Ministry* (Washington, D.C.: Alban Institute, 1977), pp. 57–60.

18. Ibid., pp. 68–69.

19. Ibid., Ch. 6, identifies the strengths and weaknesses of all four styles of influence.

Chapter 3. RESPONSE TO SOCIAL CRISIS

1. Langdon Gilkey, *Reaping the Whirlwind: A Christian Interpretation of History* (Seabury Press, 1976), p. 7.

2. Victor C. Ferkiss, *Futurology: Promise, Performance, Prospects* (Sage Publications, 1977), p. 9.

3. Ibid., p. 14.

4. Cf. Richard Falk, "Satisfying Human Needs in a World of Sovereign States: Rhetoric, Reality, and Vision," in Joseph Gremillion and William Ryan, eds., *World Faiths and the New World Order* (Washington, D.C.: Interreligious Peace Colloquium, 1978), pp. 114–115.

5. Peter Drucker, *The Age of Discontinuity* (Harper & Row, 1968), p. 10.

6. J. den Uyl, "Symposium on New International Economic Order" (The Hague: Ministry of Foreign Affairs, n.d.), p. 3.

7. Denis A. Goulet, "Ethical Struggles in the Struggle for World Development," in *Global Justice and Development*, Report of the Aspen Interreligious Consultation (Overseas Development Council, 1975), p. 45.

8. Robert Lekachman, "Looking for the Left," *Harper's*, April 1979, p. 11.

9. Ibid., p. 23.

10. Gustavo Lagos, "The Revolution of Being," in Saul

H. Menlovitz, ed., *On the Creation of a Just World Order; Preferred Worlds for the 1990's* (Free Press, 1975), p. 78, table 4.

11. Harvey Seifert, "Conditions and Dynamics in American Society," in Dieter Hessel, ed., *Rethinking Social Ministry*, p. 11.

12. Herbert Marcuse, *One Dimensional Man* (Beacon Press, 1964), p. 79.

13. Adapted from Lagos, "The Revolution of Being," pp. 81–82. From the viewpoint of ecumenical Christian ethics, compare and evaluate some other broad-gauged social analyses, e.g.: Harlan Cleveland and Thomas Wilson, Jr., *Humangrowth* (Aspen Institute for Humanistic Studies, 1978); Alvin Toffler, *The Third Wave* (Bantam Books, 1980, 1981); and Joe Holland and Peter Henriot, S.J., *Social Analysis: Linking Faith and Justice* (Washington, D.C.: Center of Concern, 1980), Ch. 4 of which portrays a "radical pastoral response" to the social conditions created by "National Security Industrial Capitalism."

14. Juan Luis Segundo, *The Hidden Motives of Pastoral Action*, tr. by John Drury (Orbis Books, 1978), pp. 33–34.

15. Compare these qualities of faithfulness with six qualities of "living shalom" that are the focus of *Teaching Toward a Faithful Vision: Shalom* (Nashville: Discipleship Resources, 1977): (1) understanding the biblical vision of shalom, (2) participating in creative change that enhances justice and peace, (3) valuing all people and serving human needs, (4) caring for and sharing the world's resources, (5) using conflict creatively and one's influence intentionally, (6) choosing to live for shalom.

16. Dietrich Bonhoeffer, *Letters and Papers from Prison*, The Enlarged Edition (Macmillian Co., 1972), p. 17.

17. John C. Haughey, "Jesus the Justice of God," in John C. Haughey, ed., *The Faith That Does Justice* (Paulist Press, 1977), p. 285.

18. Robert McAfee Brown, *Theology in a New Key: Responding to Liberation Themes* (Westminster Press, 1978), Ch. 2.

19. William E. Gibson, "A Lifestyle of Christian Faith-

fulness," in Dieter T. Hessel, ed., *Beyond Survival: Bread and Justice in Christian Perspective* (Friendship Press, 1977), p. 122.

20. Ibid., p. 129.

21. Julio de Santa Ana, *Good News to the Poor: The Challenge of the Poor in the History of the Church*, tr. by Helen Whittle (Geneva: World Council of Churches, 1977), p. 33.

22. Letty M. Russell, *Human Liberation in a Feminist Perspective—A Theology* (Westminster Press, 1974), pp. 29–30.

23. Dieter Hessel, "Eco-justice in the Eighties," in Dieter T. Hessel, ed., *Energy Ethics: A Christian Response* (Friendship Press, 1979), Ch. 1. Cf. Odil Hannes Steck, *World and Environment* (Abingdon Press, 1980).

24. Charles Birch, "Nature, Humanity and God in Ecological Perspective," a paper presented to the WCC Conference on Faith, Science, and the Future, Cambridge, Massachusetts, July 1979.

25. Herman E. Daly, "The Ecological and Moral Necessity for Limiting Economic Growth," a paper presented to the WCC Conference on Faith, Science, and the Future, July 1979.

26. E. F. Schumacher, *Small Is Beautiful: Economics as if People Mattered* (Harper & Row, 1973), p. 34.

27. Donald Shriver, "Questions Christians Ask About World Hunger," in Dieter Hessel, ed., *Beyond Survival*, p. 191.

28. Richard Barnet, "History of the Arms Race, 1945–1978," in Jane Rockman, ed., *Peace in Search of Makers* (Judson Press, 1979), pp. 12ff.

29. George Hunsinger, *Idolatry and Prayer: The Arms Race in Theological Perspective* (New York: The Riverside Church, 1978).

30. Robert McAfee Brown, *Religion and Violence: A Primer for White Americans* (Westminster Press, 1973), Chs. 5 and 6.

31. Robert Benne and Philip Hefner, *Defining America: A Christian Critique of the American Dream* (Fortress Press, 1974), pp. 111–112.

32. Gibson, "A Lifestyle of Christian Faithfulness," p. 137.

33. Robert Evans, "The Quest for Community," *Union Seminary Quarterly Review*, Winter-Summer 1975, pp. 195–197.

Chapter 4. SOCIAL DIMENSIONS OF LITURGY

1. Part of the Palm Sunday Liturgy, First United Methodist Church of Germantown, Philadelphia, Pa.

2. Bonhoeffer, *Letters and Papers from Prison*, p. 300. "Doing justice" has been substituted for the phrase "righteous action among men."

3. Bruce C. Birch and Larry L. Rasmussen, *The Predicament of the Prosperous* (Biblical Perspectives on Current Issues) (Westminster Press, 1978), p. 188.

4. Massey H. Shepherd, Jr., *Liturgy and Education* (Seabury Press, 1965), pp. 88–89.

5. Cf. Barbara Withers, ed., *Language About God in Liturgy and Scripture* (Geneva Press, 1980); Leonard Swidler, *Biblical Affirmations of Woman* (Westminster Press, 1979); Ruth Duck and Michael Bausch, eds., *Everflowing Streams: Songs for Worship* (Pilgrim Press, 1981); Marianne Sawicki, *Faith and Sexism* (Seabury Press, 1979).

6. Parker J. Palmer, *Going Public: A Working Paper for Christians on the Renewal of Public Life* (Washington, D.C.: Alban Institute, 1980), p. 8. This monograph is the basis for his recent book, *The Company of Strangers* (Crossroads Publishing Co., 1981).

7. Adapted from *Let's Worship*: A Handbook prepared by the Worship Committee for the Fifth Assembly of the World Council of Churches (RISK, 1975, 1977), pp. 43–44. Cf. Justo and Catherine Gonzalez, *In Accord: Let Us Worship* (Friendship Press, 1981).

8. Dorothee Soelle, "Cross and Class," in Dieter Hessel, ed., *Rethinking Social Ministry*, p. 31.

9. Francis Ringer, "An Experience with Base Communities in Latin America," in Dieter Hessel, ed., *Rethinking Social Ministry*, p. 45.

10. William H. Willimon, *Worship as Pastoral Care* (Abingdon Press, 1979), p. 85.

11. John Calvin, *Institutes* III. xx. 2. Cf. an unpublished dissertation by Raymond K. Anderson of Wilson College, "Love and Order: The Life-Structuring Dynamics of Grace and Virtue in Calvin's Ethical Thought" (University of Basel, 1973), Ch. 6.

Chapter 5. LIBERATING BIBLE STUDY AND PREACHING

1. Calvin, *Institutes* III. ii. 7.

2. Adapted from a 1979 lecture by Philip Wogaman, dean of Wesley Seminary, Washington, D.C.

3. Henry Mitchell, *Black Preaching* (Harper & Row, 1979).

4. George Mendenhall, "The Hebrew Conquest of Palestine," *The Biblical Archeologist*, Vol. XXV (1962), pp. 67–71; and Norman K. Gottwald, *The Tribes of Israel: A Sociology of the Religion of Liberated Israel, 1250–1000 B.C.* (Orbis Books, 1979). Gottwald's work exposes the unique socioeconomic as well as religious roots of the Judeo-Christian tradition.

5. Cf. Walter Brueggemann, *The Land* (Fortress Press, 1977), and *The Prophetic Imagination* (Fortress Press, 1978); and George Pixley, *God's Kingdom: A Guide to Bible Study* (Orbis Books, 1981).

6. James A. Sanders, "Hermeneutics," *The Interpreter's Dictionary of the Bible*, Supplementary Volume (Abingdon Press, 1976), p. 406.

7. Ibid., p. 407.

8. Howard Clark Kee, *Christian Origins in Sociological Perspective* (Westminster Press, 1980), pp. 42, 85. Cf. Howard Clark Kee, *Community of the New Age: Studies in Mark's Gospel* (Westminster Press, 1977), a study of the alienated impoverished people who produced the Gospel of Mark.

9. Tom Hanks, "Why People Are Poor (According to Scripture)," *Seeds* (Southern Baptists Concerned About World Hunger), April 1981, p. 7.

10. Brown, *Theology in a New Key*, pp. 81, 97.

11. Walter Wink, "How I Have Been Snagged by the Seat of My Pants While Reading the Bible," *The Christian Century*, Sept. 24, 1975, p. 819.

12. Walter Wink, *Transforming Bible Study* (Abingdon Press, 1980).

13. Letty M. Russell, *The Future of Partnership* (Westminster Press, 1979), p. 173.

14. Suggested by Justo and Catherine Gonzalez, *Liberation Preaching* (Abingdon Press, 1980), Ch. V.

15. To illumine a liberating social hermeneutic, I commissioned and am editing *Social Themes of the Christian Year*, a collection of essays by biblical scholars and theological ethicists on clusters of texts in the ecumenical lectionary. Another example of social interpretation keyed to the lectionary is *Third World Sermon Notes*, a quarterly subscription series edited by Walter Owensby, IDEA, 1121 University Avenue. Madison, Wisc. 53715.

Chapter 6. The Church as an Educating Community

1. Barbara Hargrove, "The Church as an Educative Force," *Connexion* (United Ministries in Education), Spring 1980, p. 7.

2. Oscar J. Hussel, "Teaching Christian Education: A Broader Concept," *The Presbyterian Outlook*, March 10, 1980, p. 6.

3. Paulo Freire, *Pedagogy of the Oppressed* (Seabury Press, 1978), p. 75.

4. Cf. Brian Wren, *Education for Justice: Pedagogical Principles* (Orbis Books, 1977), and the review by Beverly Harrison in *Union Seminary Quarterly Review*, Vol. 33, Nos. 3 and 4 (Spring and Summer 1978), pp. 215–16.

5. Birch and Rasmussen, *The Predicament of the Prosperous*, pp. 57–58.

6. Thomas Groome, *Christian Religious Education: Sharing Our Story and Vision* (Harper & Row, 1980), discusses five moments in an educational process of "shared praxis" : people (1) describe some aspect of their present action, (2) "reflect on why they do what they do" and the likely consequences of it, (3) are confronted with

some aspects of the Story and its Vision as they pertain to the present action described and analyzed, (4) "are invited to appropriate the Story to their lives in dialectic with their own stories," and (5) are given "an opportunity to choose a personal faith response for the future." But Groome's process does not develop the social dimensions and action intentions of Christian education.

7. John H. Westerhoff, III, *Inner Growth/Outer Change: An Educational Guide to Church Renewal* (Seabury Press, 1979), Ch. 11; *Tomorrow's Church: A Community of Change* (Word Books, 1976); and "The Challenge: Understanding the Problem of Faithfulness," in John Westerhoff, III, and O. C. Edwards, Jr., *A Faithful Church: Issues in the History of Catechesis* (Morehouse-Barlow Co., 1981), Ch. 1.

8. The four aspects of education for peacemaking are adapted from a lecture by Harvey Seifert. Cf. John C. Bennett and Harvey Seifert, *U.S. Foreign Policy and Christian Ethics* (Westminster Press, 1977).

9. Cf. James and Kathleen McGinnis, *Parenting for Peace and Justice* (Orbis Books, 1981), Ch. 7.

Chapter 7. RESOCIALIZING PASTORAL CARE AND LAY MINISTRY

1. Willimon, *Worship as Pastoral Care*, pp. 39–40.

2. E. Mansell Pattison, M.D., "Systems Pastoral Care," *The Journal of Pastoral Care*, Vol. 26, No. 1 (March 1972).

3. T. Richard Snyder, "Training Urban Protestant Clergy," *JSAC Grapevine*, Vol. 11, No. 9 (April 1980).

4. Ernesto Cardenal, *The Gospel in Solentiname*, Vol. 3 (Orbis Books, 1979), pp. 195ff., offers a lively grass-roots dialogue on the meaning of John 10:7–16.

5. William E. Gibson, *A Covenant Group for Lifestyle Assessment: Participant's Manual*, Rev. Ed. (Program Agency, The United Presbyterian Church U.S.A., 1981). A related curriculum *Lifestyle Change for Children*, by Doris L. Shettel, may be used in family and intergenerational settings. Ordering address in Preface, note 1.

6. Donald Browning, "The Moral Context of Pastoral Care," in Dieter Hessel, ed., *Rethinking Social Ministry*, pp. 73–74.

7. John Fish, "Social Justice and the Serviced Society," in Dieter Hessel, ed., *Rethinking Social Ministry*, pp. 23–24.

8. Cf. Dieter Hessel and George Wilson, *Congregational Lifestyle Change for the Lean Years* (Program Agency, The United Presbyterian Church U.S.A., 1981).

9. Karen McLean Hessel and Dieter T. Hessel, "Women in Social Ministry," in Dieter Hessel, ed., *Rethinking Social Ministry*, pp. 57–58.

10. John H. Hendrickson, "Mutual Ministry," a paper circulated by Auburn Seminary and reprinted in Dieter Hessel and Wilson, *Congregational Lifestyle Change for the Lean Years*, pp. 131–132.

11. George H. Crowell, "The Social Vocation of the Laity," in Dieter Hessel, ed., *Rethinking Social Ministry*, p. 81.

12. Cameron P. Hall, *Lay Action—The Church's Third Force* (Friendship Press, 1974), pp. 22–23.

13. *A Strategy of Hope* (Metropolitan Associates of Philadelphia [MAP], 1972), p. 82.

14. Cf. Russell, *The Future of Partnership*.

15. Larry Rasmussen, *American Economic Life and Christian Faith* (Augsburg Publishing House, 1980), pp. 28–29.

16. Crowell, "The Social Vocation of the Laity," p. 85.

17. Dieter T. Hessel, ed., *The Agricultural Mission of Churches and Land-Grant Universities*, papers of the Informal Consultation on the Response of Land-Grant Universities to World Hunger convened by John T. Conner, 1978 (Iowa State University Press, 1980).

18. Mark Gibbs, "Laity on the Fringe," *A.D.*, May 1980, p. 22.

19. Crowell, "The Social Vocation of the Laity," p. 83.

Chapter 8. RENEWAL OF COMMUNITY MINISTRY

1. Cf. "How to Diagnose a Neighborhood," in Rochelle B. Warren and Donald L. Warren, *Neighborhood*

Organizer's Handbook, (University of Notre Dame Press, 1977), Ch. 8; Richard Taylor, "Discovering Your Neighborhood's Needs: A Practical Guide for Beginning Local Ministry," *Sojourners*, Nov. 1978; and "A Form for Church/Community Analysis," developed by the Inter-Seminary Theological Education for Ministry Program in New York City, reprinted in *Church and Society*, May-June 1980, pp. 73–76.

2. Cf. Dieter Hessel, ed., *Maggie Kuhn on Aging* (Westminster Press, 1977); and *Empowering Ministry in an Ageist Society*, A Princeton Seminary Symposium (Program Agency, The United Presbyterian Church U.S.A., 1981), available from Presbyterian Office on Aging, 341 Ponce de Leon Avenue, N.E., Atlanta, Ga. 30365.

3. Edward M. Huenemann, "Theological Dimensions of a Ministry of Advocacy," a presentation to the Synod of the Northeast, June 22–23, 1979.

4. Sketched by Lyle Franzen, an experienced community organizer who also teaches at Valparaiso University. Adapted for this book.

5. Edward Chambers, "Organizing for Family and Congregation" (Chicago: Industrial Areas Foundations, 1978), mimeographed.

6. Harry Fagan, *Empowerment: Skills for Parish Social Action* (Paulist Press, 1979), pp. 23, 20. The problem-issue-action chart is adapted from this manual.

7. Cf. James E. Crowfoot and Mark A. Chesler, *Comparative Perspectives on Planned Social Change* (Ann Arbor, Mich.: Community Resources, n.d.).

Chapter 9. ENGAGING IN RESPONSIBLE GOVERNANCE

1. *Chicago Tribune*, Jan. 5, 1981, Sec. I, p. 4.

2. Shriver and Ostrom, *Is There Hope for the City?* p. 116.

3. Ibid., pp. 118, 119.

4. E.g., IMPACT, 110 Maryland Avenue, N.E., Washington, D.C. 20002; and Bread for the World, 32 Union Square East, New York, N.Y. 10003. Cf. Jack Corbett and Elizabeth Smith, *Becoming a Prophetic Community* (John Knox Press, 1980), pp. 65–71. Models for community

service and advocacy are summarized in Part Two of their book. For an explanation of how denominational staff in Washington participate in legislative action, see Paul Kittlaus, "The Churches Policy Advocacy," *Church and Society*, Sept.-Oct. 1980, pp. 24–30.

5. *The Church's Responsibility in Society*, a statement of the 1972 General Assembly (UPCUSA), and my *Reconciliation and Conflict: Church Controversy Over Social Involvement*.

6. Walter Wink, "Unmasking the Powers: Economics in Biblical Perspective," *Sojourners*, Oct. 1978.

7. Henry B. Schacht, "Responsibility at Cummins—A Commitment in Search of an Institutional Arrangement," an address to executives in Minneapolis, n.d.

8. Adaptation of a case study suggested by W. Stewart MacColl, a United Presbyterian pastor in Houston, Texas, and former chairperson of the denomination's Committee on Mission Responsibility Through Investment.

9. David J. Kalke, "Unmasking the Strategies of Multinational Corporations," *The Witness*, Vol. 63, No. 1 (Jan. 1980), pp. 8–9.

10. Henry Clark, *Ministries of Dialogue: The Church Confronts the Power Structure* (Association Press, 1971), did a careful analysis of the industrial mission movement in its heyday. Many of these specialized ministries were reduced to impotence during the 1970's.

11. Helpful information is available in David Vogel, *Lobbying the Corporation* (Basic Books, 1973), and the publications of Corporate Data Exchange, 198 Broadway, Room 707, New York, N.Y. 10038; Council on Economic Priorities, 84 Fifth Avenue, New York, N.Y. 10011; Interfaith Center on Corporate Responsibility, 475 Riverside Drive, Room 566, New York, N.Y. 10115; Investor Responsibility Research Center, 1522 K St., N.W., Suite 730, Washington, D.C. 20005.

Chapter 10. ACTIVE FORMS OF THE CHURCH

1. The illustration was submitted by and discussed with Douglas E. Bartlett, pastor of Good Shepherd United

Presbyterian Church, Commack, New York.

2. A well-developed strategy of "Social Ministry Around Employment," utilizing this multi-mode model appears in *Justice Ministries*, Summer 1980, pp. 40–64. (Institute on the Church in Urban-Industrial Society, 5700 S. Woodlawn Avenue, Chicago, Ill. 60637.)

3. Guidance in strategic action planning is available in Fagan, *Empowerment: Skills for Parish Social Action,* and Dieter Hessel, *A Social Action Primer* (Westminster Press, 1972).

4. Ringer, "An Experience with Base Communities in Latin America," pp. 45–46. Also see several articles on base communities in *Christianity and Crisis*, Sept. 21, 1981.

5. The results were published in an occasional paper (now out of print), by Dieter Hessel and Les Galbraith, *Socially Involved Congregations* (Philadelphia: Board of Christian Education, The United Presbyterian Church U.S.A., 1971), pp. 16–28.

6. Cf. George M. Wilson, "Justice-Oriented Congregations," in Dieter Hessel, ed., *Rethinking Social Ministry*, pp. 51–55, and articles written by leaders of these congregations in Dieter Hessel and Wilson, *Congregational Lifestyle Change for the Lean Years.*

7. Carl S. Dudley, "Measuring Church Growth," *The Christian Century*, June 6–13, 1979, p. 638.

8. C. Peter Wagner, *Our Kind of People* (John Knox Press, 1979). A critical review, entitled "Evangelism Without the Gospel," appeared in *Sojourners*, Feb. 1980.

9. Carl Dudley, "Social Involvement/Church Growth," in Dieter Hessel, ed., *Participant's Notebook for Social Ministry Institutes* (Program Agency, The United Presbyterian Church U.S.A., 1980), summarizes recent studies of congregations in the United Church of Christ, The United Methodist Church, and The United Presbyterian Church U.S.A.

10. Harvey Seifert, "Conditions and Dynamics in American Society," in Dieter Hessel, ed., *Rethinking Social Ministry*, p. 10.

11. Dudley, "Social Involvement/Church Growth."

12. Davidson et al., "Increasing Church Involvement in Social Concerns," p. 294.

13. Everett L. Perry and Dean R. Hoge, "Faith Priorities of Pastor and Laity as a Factor in the Growth or Decline of Presbyterian Congregations," *Review of Religious Research*, Vol. 22, No. 3 (March 1981), p. 229.

14. Ibid., p. 231.

15. These principles are adapted from work sheets used in Social Ministry Institutes, prepared by Harvey Seifert, Emeritus Professor of Christian Ethics, School of Theology at Claremont, California. Cf. Donald E. Bossart, *Creative Conflict in Religious Education and Church Administration* (Religious Education Press, 1980).

Index of Scripture References

Index of Subjects and Names